YOUT 201

Student Work Text

Connecting students with Jesus Christ, their families, their ministry, their church, and their generation.

YOUT 201 – Survey of Youth Ministries

An Introductory Course for Today's Student Ministries

Dr. Richard S. Brown, Jr.

Liberty University
1971 University Blvd.
Lynchburg, VA 24502
Phone 434.582.2310
rsbrown@liberty.edu

Academx
Publishing Services

TABLE OF CONTENTS

The Five Relational Priorities of Student Ministry
A student ministry should be connecting students with Jesus Christ, their families, their ministry, their church, and their generation.

The Five Principled Priorities of Student Ministry
Christ-centered, purpose-driven, family-friendly, team-oriented, church-connected

Unless otherwise noted, all Scriptures are taken from the New International Version

A Special Thanks to Doug Randlett

"I want to thank Pastor Doug Randlett, my youth ministry professor, for everything you taught me about student ministry. It was under your instruction that I was first exposed to the knowledge of student ministry. Yet it was more than knowledge I gained from you; I gained from you your excitement, heart, and life. It was this very course that God used to capture my heart for students and the ministry of the church's role in reaching and discipling students. As I took this course in the spring of 1983, God confirmed in me His calling of student ministry in my own life.

Upon graduation from the youth ministry department from Liberty University I continued to draw upon your teaching and example as I journeyed through my own years of ministry. I cannot remember how many times I would recall and apply the various aspects to ministry which you taught all of us. The Lord only knows the multiplicity of your ministry through my life as well as hundreds of other Liberty students, as we have left this university to engage Jesus Christ into the lives of so many teenagers.

I was humbled as I returned to Liberty in 2003 to teach the youth ministry courses I took from you. I was even more humbled to realize my new office was the office you once occupied, including the old wooden desk. Now as I have redeveloped the course you developed almost thirty years ago, I face this opportunity with excitement yet caution. I only want to enhance to a new generation of student ministry workers what you have so effectively done for almost three complete decades. I trust you will be pleased; that student ministry workers will become competent, surrendered servants of our great King; and the majesty of Jesus Christ will be radiantly evidenced as His work goes forward for years to come.

As you are now one of my pastors at Thomas Road Baptist Church, you will always be my youth ministry professor. For this I am eternally indebted."

INTRODUCTION:

The Presuppositions to this Course

What You Need to Know Before Starting This Course

Section Headings:

Learning Outcomes:

In this chapter the student will…

- *be introduced to the professor and his desire for healthy student ministries.*

- *see the methods the professor will use in laying out this course.*

- *understand the direction, expectations, and definition of terms for the course.*

ABOUT THE AUTHOR

Richard Brown has been active in student ministry since 1983 and entered full time ministry as a youth pastor upon graduation from Liberty University in 1985. It was during college that God called him and equipped him for vocational youth ministry where he majored in youth ministries. It was also during this time he met his lifetime love, friend, mate, and partner in ministry. He and his wife Janet have served together in churches in the Midwest and the Seattle area. In 2003, Rich transitioned from local church student ministry to "come home" to his alma mater to become a professor within the school's Department of Church Ministries. He now teaches many of the youth ministry courses he took as a student, including this course. While he still misses "being" a youth pastor, he is blessed to be educating the next generation of youth leaders and has a deep love and respect for college students. His wife, Janet, is also an L.U. alumnus and is currently a professor at Liberty University. They have three adult children: Rich III, Jenna, and Ryan.

Whenever Dr. Brown speaks to a group; he typically starts by saying to the audience they need to know where he is coming from.

- *There is ONE God (and it's not us!).*
- *God's Word is absolute truth!*
- *Jesus Christ is LORD!*
- *Salvation is based on 0% us and 100% God.*
- *We are called to repent of our sins and lay ourselves before the Lord, receiving His grace for forgiveness and become His followers.*
- *Middle School and High School students are a vital part of today's church.*
- *Students are the key players in reaching their generation.*
- *We as adults MUST be highly engaged in their lives.*

ABOUT THE CONTENT IN THE WORK TEXT

1. This work text is used both in the residential and online YOUT 201.

This work text was originally developed for the residential course; however, this material is also used online. In doing this, the intention is to maintain the integrity of the course for students in both programs. While each student may be at a different season of life, the desire is to have the principles communicated to both groups. In addition, by using the residential work text for the adult learner, the online student can have a stronger sense of being on the campus and in the classroom.

2. This work text is written from the trenches.

While most of this material is directly written by Dr. Brown and comes straight out of his own ministry experience, he ardently wants to emphasize he does not consider himself to have been a high profile youth worker. While he has been given the serious responsibility of teaching many of the youth ministry classes at Liberty, he often wonders why he was chosen to teach these classes. This material is submitted in humility and is written relationally. Dr. Brown shares, *"This work text is built with the idea of you* (the reader) *and I sitting down at Starbucks and I am simply sharing my own ministry thoughts and experiences with you. Looking back, there are things that worked and things that didn't work. While I obviously do not know everything about student ministry I do seek to be a*  *faithful component of this God-given chain of ministry training (2 Timothy 2:2). I do NOT want to create 'little Doc Brown's' running around ... I want creative, students willing to invade the darkness of today's student culture with God's glorious light using the gifts and abilities God has given each of them."* And if each student does this, Dr. Brown believes he will have done his job effectively.

3. This Material is Bible Packed!!!

One of his great concerns within current youth ministry is an apparent shift away from biblical principles and movement toward relevance and/or experience as the foundations to ministry. The core of this material is the Word of God. *"Our commitment to the Bible is what should separate Christian youth ministries from the culture's youth organizations. Whereas they may base their philosophy and approach on pragmatic, politically-correct ideals, we must base ours on the ever-relevant, yet never-changing principles of the Word of God. Jesus Christ is Lord and He is the owner of the ministry and these students. I was simply put in this position to carry out HIS work. The more I study the Word of God, especially the life of Jesus Christ, the more confident I become that God's Word is the best student ministry book ever written. Therefore, I will use His training material in this training material."*

4. This Material Is Original to this Course.

While Dr. Brown realizes so much of what he has learned is a compilation of others, he wants to preface this work text by communicating the material in this manual, unless otherwise noted, is his own original work with much of it coming out of his own ministry experience. Throughout the work text there may be reference to other student ministry resources. When outside sources are used, he will provide reference to the various outside sources. He seeks to be above reproach when using outside material.

"God is so good to provide resources in our life to bring us to maturity in ministry. If we are wise and pay attention, we all will learn ministry from so many sources: our great Teacher and His Ministry Manual, the gift of people who touch our lives, those that mentor us from a distance, and life itself. While I owe so much of who I am to those who have influenced me, the information in this work text is directly written by me. While the basic concepts of ministry are by no means new, the acronyms, ministry definitions, and all of the material in this booklet, unless otherwise noted, are original. For those of you who are aware of various youth ministry books of recent years, some of this may sound like I simply copied others and reworded it. I can honestly say what you are about to read was developed in the mid to late 1980's, years before I ever heard of various youth structures which are common place today. In no way is there any plagiarism or wrong doing. It was designed on a pad of paper before there was an iPad!"

While much of the material may have formulated in the 1980's and 1990's, the reader must understand this has nothing to do with being stuck "back in the day." The principles are timeless. They are to be like a foundational rock. Yet the translating of these principles to current and future generations must always be fresh and understandable to a new generation. Therefore, while the principles in this book may be tried and true, there will also be content (research, statistics, trends, etc.) which is as current to the time of writing as possible.

5. This Material Is Principle-Oriented, not Program-Oriented.

"As a young youth pastor I would read every youth book I could get my hands on. In many cases I would feel like I could not identify with the author of the book. Most of the youth books I read were written from youth pastors and workers who were in churches larger than my home town of 1000 residents. While the principles they taught were good, in many cases I would feel inadequate, even discouraged, because my ministry situation was not as big as the one in the book. This would cause me to imagine these authors/youth pastors could not possibly understand what I was going through. They have more volunteer leaders than I had students. I would think, 'I am just an average youth pastor who writes his own sermons, runs all the events, and even puts together the promotional handouts. Where are the average youth pastors that I can relate to and the needed material to help me in my situation?'"

This material has nothing to do with the <u>size</u> of the student ministry! The principles contained can be integrated into a student ministry of five, fifty, one hundred and fifty, or higher. Dr. Brown continues, *"I know this is true because over the years I had various ministries of five, fifty, and one hundred and fifty students."* This manual has nothing to do with <u>location</u> of the student ministry. *"This is also true because I served in churches in smaller cities in the Midwest and larger suburban communities of Seattle, Washington."* Finally, this material has nothing to do with the <u>economic</u> <u>situation</u> of the student ministry. *"Again, I know because I was in churches which would be labeled as lower-middle class, middle class, and upper-middle class."* The following material is not based on theory; rather, tested and proven student ministry principles. The following material will not focus on program ideas but will focus on a biblically based philosophy which transcends size, site, or situation.

6. **This Material Is a Combination of Both a Narrative Style (notes) and an Outline Style (fill-in-the-blanks).**

The material in this work text will include the standard outlines where the student fills in the notes but will also include various narrative writings. The residential student will have the answers to the blanks provided in class while the online student will find the answers in the weekly PowerPoint presentations. Dr. Brown has written this manual in the first person tense. Remember, it is like he and you are chatting at Starbucks talking about student ministry.

"Please understand the two easiest decisions I ever made were my commitments to the two 'J's' in my life: 1) Jesus Christ, my Lord and Savior and 2) Janet, my precious wife. The most difficult decision was to step aside from being a youth pastor and accept the call of God to train future youth pastors and leaders. Whenever I teach this material, I miss what I left as a youth pastor. I think you will see this and Lord willing, will catch this. My desire is to see each of you engage in the work from which God had me step aside as a pastor and begin to fill the world of the youth culture with the majesty of Jesus Christ."

ABOUT THE AUTHOR'S APPROACH TO TEACHING

1. **What the Student Can Expect From Him.**

In relation to his teaching philosophy Dr. Brown states, *"While I realize I am here to teach classes, I see my greater responsibility is to teach students. I believe ministry is about people, not programs. And if I believe this and teach this, then I better model it. When I look into the lives of my students, I see* the God-given potential in each one. I become excited considering what God can do through the future life and ministry of each student. This is why I take my job very seriously." He continues, "Being part of an academic institution, I will teach the material, provide learning outcomes, and assess these outcomes. So I will guard the professional standard of academia. But I want each student's learning process to be much more than just going through youth ministry material, studying adolescent trends, and looking into program ideas. I desire to share my personal insights and experiences as well. I want to have my life transparent before my students. What I remember so much about my youth classes at Liberty was the practical insights and personal stories of my professors. Over the years, I constantly found myself quoting different insights I gained from them so I know the power of 'real life.' While I am committed to text books and work texts, I want to weave 'real life' ministry into my teaching."

> "And the things you have heard me say in the presence of many witnesses entrust to reliable men who will also be qualified to teach others."

Dr. Brown vows to give his absolute best when teaching. He does have class and his classes will go the full period. This is his commitment to excellence and stewardship. His method of teaching is summed up in his acronym of the word "**PASS**." Based on the command of 2 Timothy 2:2 to develop leaders, it is Dr. Brown's deepest desire to pass his love and understanding of student ministry onto his students.

Provide the Information – When it comes to the course, his notes will be completely covered and all of the blanks will be filled in!

Application oriented – His lectures will be direct and engaging. He realizes only spiritually healthy youth workers can build healthy youth.

Stories to explain – He will share many stories of "back in the day" as well as current life in order to explain and cite the points being shared.

Scripture based – He realizes only the eternal Word of God is the sufficient resource needed to build the Church of Jesus Christ. He will provide many Scriptural references so be prepared to write many verses in the notes!

2. What He Expects From His Students.

While Dr. Brown will do his part, he also realizes that learning is a two way street. So much will also depend upon the student. Within his years of teaching at Liberty, he has already seen three basic approaches students have to their classes. The first approach is *"what do I have to do to just get by."* His response to this is that Jesus Christ expects His followers to be excellent in what they do. The second approach is *"what can I do to get a good grade."* This is somewhat better but he believes it is still incomplete thinking as the grade should not be the goal, rather comprehension. The third approach is *"what can I learn about student ministry that will build a foundation for my ministry career and/or better the church I will be a part of."* If this is the student's approach, great things can happen! Whether you are considering student ministry as a career or not, he seeks to find each student treating this class as a professional.

In relation to his goal for each student in this course, Dr. Brown seeks to see each student ask himself or herself the question, *"God, where is my place in the Harvest Field of students?"* While he realizes that YOUT 201 attracts many different types of college students with many different academic goals and personal motives for taking this course, he does want to see each one be open to what God has for them. He also desires to see each student have a teachable attitude while in the class. Each semester there are some who have the *"I already know all of this"* attitude. Sadly, there are others who have the *"I have to be in this class and don't really care"* attitude. Thankfully, the majority of students do approach the course with a teachable attitude and it is from this humble attitude that God can best do His work.

3. What Each Should Expect From the Other.

The three basic "house rules" Dr. Brown has for class is based on his "Three R's." What he expects from you, you can also expect from him. They are as follows:

<u>Responsibility</u> – Dr. Brown will do his best to provide the needed verbal and written communication about the course, he will have your assignments graded in a timely manner, he will respond to emails accordingly, etc. He also expects each student to fulfill their responsibilities accordingly. This includes: consistent attendance (both physically and mentally), following instructions, doing assignments correct and on time, positively participating in class, bringing the necessary materials to class and taking notes, etc.

Respect – Dr. Brown believes in creating a "safe" environment in the classroom. Your professor will not mock you or treat you as inferiors. He does not call his college students, "college kids." He realizes he is equal to his students in the eyes of God. He does not refer to others in "military" language (calling people by last names). He also realizes there is the biblical command to respect authority and expects the students to show respect to God, each other, their authorities, and to him. This includes: how one speaks to others and the professor both in attitude and actions.

Relationship – Dr. Brown seeks to know his students as persons, not as numbers. He realizes the glue of student ministry is relationships and seeks to model this in class. He longs to know each student's first name and something personal about them. With the advent of larger classes, this task is becoming harder. Please seek him out and introduce yourself continually until he knows your name. He also desires the student to know others in the class as well. Typically, the student who keeps to him/herself does not do as well as the student who becomes part of community.

The bottom line is he will treat each student like an adult and expects each student to act like an adult. This does not mean, *"You can't tell me what to do because I am an adult"* (that is considered immature). This does mean, *"You can count on me because I am responsible."*

Along with the "Three R's", his classroom core values include: passion, integrity, laughter, learning, and interaction.

CHAPTER ONE:

The Present Condition of the Student Culture

Where is today's youth culture?

Section Headings:

Learning Outcomes:

In this chapter the student will…

- *Gain insights into the reality of the spiritual condition, both within the church and outside the church.*

- *Gain insights into the reality of the social condition, both within the church and outside the church.*

Where is Today's Youth Culture?

I cannot think of a better place to start this course than having you take a look at the spiritual and social climate of today's middle school and high school students. Since the dominant age of college students who take this course residentially are 18-20 years old, most of you are not too far removed from the high school scene. While I am the "seasoned adult", I am sure you can educate me on your generation better than I can to you. Yet sometimes when one is in the forest, it is harder to see all of trees in the forest. So let's step outside the forest of the student culture and begin to see them as the Lord Jesus Christ sees them.

> "When he saw the crowds, he had compassion on them, because they were harassed and helpless, like sheep without a shepherd."
> (Matthew 9:36)

Today's Spiritual Climate

In recent years, author and speaker Josh McDowell has been traveling the nation speaking of what our students believe and how they behave. In his book *The Last Christian Generation*, Josh McDowell provides some sobering realities of today's evangelical teenagers (with much of his research derived from the Barna Research Group).

WHAT ABOUT DOCTRINE?

- ___63___ % don't believe Jesus is the Son of the one true God.
- ___58___ % believe all faiths teach equally valid truths.
- ___51___ % don't believe Jesus rose from the dead.
- ___65___ % don't believe Satan is a real entity.
- ___68___ % don't believe the Holy Spirit is a real entity.
- ___64___ % believe if a person is generally good or does enough good things for others they will earn a place in heaven.[1]

---

[1] Barna Research Group, *Third Millennium Teens* (Ventura, CA: The Barna Research Group, Ltd., 1999), 51.

90% before 18 years
64% Barna- before 18 years
13% Barna - before 21 years
23% Barna- as adults

WHAT ABOUT TRUTH AND ABSOLUTES?

- _81_ % believe all truth relates to the individual.[2]
- _72_ % say it's true if it works for you.[3]

There is no absolute truth:[4]

    1991 – _52_ %

    1994 – _62_ %

    1999 – _78_ %

    2003 – _91_ %

The Bible is the Infallible Word of God:

    1995 – _10_ %

    2002 – _4_ %

> **Is the United States a "Christian" Nation?**
>
> **Would you say that we as followers of Christ are no longer the "home" team?**

WHAT ABOUT SALVATION?

What age are most people saved?

For the past few decades the consensus among evangelicals was typically _90_ % of those who come to Jesus Christ will do so before the age of 18. According to pollster George Barna, more recent research would indicate that _64_ % of believers receive Christ before the age of 18 while _13_ % more receive Christ before 21 year of age. This leaves us with _23_ % of believers coming to Christ as adults.[5] Whether it is the traditional number of 90% saved prior to 18 or Barna's 77% saved before 21, I trust you can see if one is going to enter the Kingdom it will be done in the early years of one's life.

How many students are saved?

First of all, _only God_ knows yet there is some research to give us a hint. Interestingly, in 1960 Youth For Christ did a survey which stated only _5_ % of students stated they had a "Christian conversion experience", _35_ % claimed to have some type of religious affiliation, and _60_ % considered themselves unchurched.[6] During the early 1990's I read of a Youth for Christ survey which revealed that among high school students _33_ % considered themselves "born again." Yet the majority of the 33% (27 out of 33) considered being born again as a "gradual" process

---

[2] Ibid, 49.

[3] Ibid, 49.

[4] The statistics were from a live presentation by Josh McDowell at Thomas Road Baptist Church and Liberty University in October, 2007 in Lynchburg, Virginia.

[5] Goerge Barna, *Evangelism Is Most Effective Among Kids* http://www.barna.org/FlexPage.aspx?Page=BarnaUpdate&BarnaUpdateID=172

[6] Mark H. Senter III, *The Coming Revolution in Youth Ministry* (Wheaton: Victor Books, 1992), 129-30.

of works. The remaining stated that "born again" was a faith based relationship with Jesus Christ. This meant only __6__ out of 100 were claiming Christ based on their faith in His work, not their work. Currently the newest Christian research (Thom Rainer, George Barna, among others) indicates this number has moved to 4%! This means only ___4___ in 100 teenagers in this nation say they are born again (as defined by grace). If these statistics are anything close to reality, this indicates that for over fifty years less than 10% of the youth culture claims a saving relationship with Jesus Christ.

WHAT ABOUT CHURCH?

How about students "sticking around" church?

Many years ago during my first youth ministry, I heard Josh McDowell speak at Chicago's Moody Church. Josh reported that ___90___% of evangelical young people left the church with less than 20% ever returning. That was 1987. Over the years other evangelical leaders and pollsters have done the same research with similar results. For over thirty years, the church of Jesus Christ has consistently been losing many of its youth.

Why is the church losing so many of its own students? (That's in chapter seven!)

I understand there will be those who will downplay this information and would argue that I am sensationalizing, even fabricating the situation. During my doctoral research I read an article from *Christianity Today* in which the writer challenges some of the statistics we have just examined.[7] The article suggests reservation of such numbers and sarcastically implies fabrication of these statistics for manipulation purposes. I will be honest. As already stated, when it comes to statistics, only God Himself truly knows the numbers. But I do want to raise a few questions:

> *What is the definition of one being a Christian?*
> *Are there any real life gauges that can indicate "real" numbers?*
> *Why are so many churches dying and many actually closing up?*
> *Can the abandonment of Christianity happen in America?*

Again, I understand there will be those who will downplay or even disregard this departure from the church. I want you do investigate this for yourself. Here is a simple personal test – consider

---

[7] William R. Kenan, Jr. *Evangelicals Behaving Badly with Statistics* http://www.christianitytoday.com/bc/2007/001/5.11.html

your own church and churches you are familiar with. The attendance of "twenty something's" will be a visible indicator. As you do your research, note that according to the 2012 U.S. Census Bureau, there were 42,771,000 adults between the ages of 20–29. This is 14.2% of the total United States population[8]. Does your church this Sunday have 14% of its attending population between 20-29 years of age? If so, then this means you are simply reaching the average number of this age group and most of your church's adolescents stayed in church. Yet if this number is less, there may be an issue.

(I am aware that some churches have a focus of reaching out to the millennials, almost to the exclusion of older adults. This is a different conversation but I am specifically considering the traditional multigenerational church when using this model.)

> The next time you see a large group of teenagers, for each 100 you see, only 4 claim personal faith in Jesus Christ.

Sometime when you are at the mall, just grab a refreshing beverage and sit in the main hallway or food court and simply watch the youth that pass you by. As you see these teenagers, look into their faces and be reminded that Jesus Christ made them to know Him and to worship Him (Colossians 1:16).

Let's Review...

- 77-85% of all Christians receive Christ before high school graduation!
- Only 4% of today's students claim a "faith alone" salvation relationship with Jesus Christ!
- Up to 85% of evangelical youth "drop out" of church between 10th – 12th grades!
- Putting these together, consider that at each typical public high school graduation, for every 100 students you see, only 1 claims a personal "faith alone" relationship with Jesus Christ and is still actively attending church.

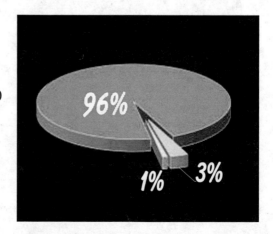

---

[8] http://www.census.gov/population/age/data/2012comp.html

Going back to the same census, there were 41,844,000 youth between the ages of 10–19. This is 14% of the total United States population[9]. When one factors in the 96% unsaved statistic, this means we are looking at 40,170,242 adolescents who are in darkness and need Christ. This leaves us with 1, 673,760 students who claim salvation in Christ. Even of you consider losing 75% (which is lower than some research); this leaves the church with 418,440 students to reach over 40 million. Sounds like Gideon numbers to me! Church, we have our work before us.

Think about this...
Are Students the "Church of Tomorrow"?

(Have you ever heard the line "teenagers are the church of tomorrow"? Think about it ... if the church keeps telling students they are the church of tomorrow, maybe they will take us up on it and say "see ya tomorrow"!)

Today's Social Climate

WHAT IS THEIR SOCIAL CHARACTER? (Indicators _____ – WHO THEY ARE)

ACTIONS:	ATTITUDES:
1.	1.
2.	2.
3.	3.
4.	4.
5.	5.
6.	6.
7.	7.
8.	8.
9.	9.
10.	10.

[9] http://www.census.gov/population/age/data/2012comp.html

Do you think there is any correlation between one's attitudes and their actions?

> Jesus Christ stated, "For out of the heart come evil thoughts, murder, adultery, sexual immorality, theft, false testimony, slander" (Matthew 15:19)

Think About This! When reading this prophetic passage from 2 Timothy 3:1-5, see if you recognize today's student culture in any of these areas?

1 "But mark this: There will be terrible times in the last days. 2 People will be lovers of themselves, lovers of money, boastful, proud, abusive, disobedient to their parents, ungrateful, unholy, 3 without love, unforgiving, slanderous, without self-control, brutal, not lovers of the good, 4 treacherous, rash, conceited, lovers of pleasure rather than lovers of God— 5 having a form of godliness but denying its power. Have nothing to do with them."

While these sins have always been around, it is my opinion they seem more prevalent today than in previous years. I know some of you may think that humankind has always been depraved. While this is true, the Scriptures do speak of the fluidity of spiritual climate, both seen in individuals and in nations. Read Judges as well as the historical books in the Old Testament. Cultures do go through moral decay and hopefully repentance and restoration. Your observation assignment in this course will be a chance for you to see the adolescent culture up close and personal.

Unless you looked here before giving your answers in the above table, my hunch is the class would have focused on the negative actions and attitudes of today's students. What are some of the positive behaviors you have seen in today's adolescents?_____
_____
_____
_____

WHAT ARE THEIR SOCIAL COMPONENTS? (Ingredients – WHAT MAKES THEM)

Before you consider my thoughts, take a moment and write in your own thought. What social structures or social areas go into the makeup of a teenager? When you discover mine, keep in mind I am not suggesting a ranking order of priority, rather a simple list.

YOUR THOUGHTS:	MY THOUGHTS:
1.	1. Entertainment (music, movies, television, internet, video games)
2.	2. Peer relationships
3.	③ Other's opinions
4.	4. need for intimacy
5.	5. Busyness
6.	6. Ethnicity
7.	7. Economic Situation (toys, clothes)
8.	8. Geographical Location
9.	9. World view (school, religion, politics)
10.	10. parents

Think back to when you were young - which components did you think then were critical and/or instrumental in your own adolescent beliefs and behaviors?

Think now as an adult – which of these ingredients you now realize had significant influence on your adolescent beliefs and behaviors?

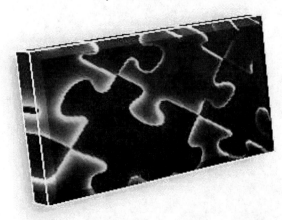

WE SEEM TO BE A HUMAN ASSEMBLY OF MANY FACTORS WHICH MAKE US INTO WHO WE ARE.

WHAT ARE THEIR SOCIAL CLUSTERS? (I<u>dentity</u> – WHO THEY ACT LIKE)

Ahhh…the School Lunch Room!

Assemble the "Groups" at your school as to where they sat in the lunch room! (I started it – you finish it!)

Athletes	Cheerleaders	Hipsters	Choir Kids

Questions to Consider:

Does "Where you sit at lunch" matter to students??? If so, why? (<u>Status</u>, <u>significance</u>, <u>security</u> *)*

What would happen if you got "bumped" from a lunch table? (<u>rejection</u>, <u>isolation</u> *)*

How important to the student is the social group they spend time with? (<u>influence</u> *)*

How important to God is the social group that a Christian student spends time with? (<u>Psalm</u> *1;* <u>Proverbs</u> *1; 1* <u>Corinthians</u> *15:33-34)*

Million Dollar Question…where do you think Jesus would go hang out?

Christian psychologist Dr. Les Parrot provides a listing of five areas where adolescents search for identity[10] As you consider these, write some examples next to the specific area.

1. **Through status** _symbols_ - _____
2. **Through forbidden** _behaviors_ _____
3. **Through** _rebellion_ - _____
4. **Through** _idols_ . - _____
5. **Through cliquish** _exclusion_ - _____

When honored to speak at various student ministries, one of the topics I enjoy speaking on is our identity being found in Christ. When you see the verse below (Colossians 1:16) you see Who made us (which gives our identity) and why He made us (which gives our purpose). My value is not found in what I think of me ("self-esteem") or what others think of me (performance); it is what my Maker and Master thinks of me. There is freedom in this truth!

Where Does Jesus Fit In?

Colossians 1:16 "For by him all things were created: things in heaven and on earth, visible and invisible, whether thrones or powers or rulers or authorities; all things were created **by him** and **for him**."

Colossians 2:10 "and you have been given fullness in Christ, who is the head over every power and authority."

2 Corinthians 3:4-5 "Such confidence as this is ours through Christ before God. 5Not that we are competent in ourselves to claim anything for ourselves, but our competence comes from God."

Let's help students find their identity, purpose, completeness, and confidence must come from the One who made them!

---

[10] Les Parrot, *Helping the Struggling Adolescents: A Guide to Thirty-six Common Problems for Counselors, Pastors and Youth Workers* (Grand Rapids, Zondervan, 2000), 19-21.

WHAT ARE THEIR SOCIAL CHROMOSOMES? (I_Influence_ – WHO THEY BECOME)

- _Home_ (Parents, siblings, family history)
- _Community_ (where they live, school, work, organizations, church, etc...)
- _Relationships_ (friends, mentors, relatives, etc...)

> **You will learn much about the social behavior of today's students as you fulfill your "Cultural Observation Project."**

WHAT ARE THEIR SOCIAL CONCERNS? (I_mportance_ – WHAT MATTERS MOST)

As you consider these, please note the paradox. My point is that adolescence is a growing, stretching and confusing time.

1. **They want R**_eality_**(How? / Why?)**

   ...yet doesn't it seem even the reality shows seem a little fake, complete with the star "Drama Queen" playing up to the camera?

2. **They want R**_elationships_ **(How? / Why?)**

   ...yet doesn't it seem that students' idea of "communication" is impersonal (electronic; i.e. social media connection such as texting, Instagram, Twitter, Facebook, etc.) and the content is often shallow?

3. **They want R**_espect_ **(How? / Why?)**

   ...yet doesn't it seem there is such a disregard for authority, property, others, and human life?

4. **They want R**_easons_ **(How? / Why?)**

   ...yet doesn't it seem like when given a "factual" (objective) reason, there can be a "feeling" (subjective) rebuttal ("yeah, well that's just your opinion...")?

5. **They want R**_ecognition_ **(How? / Why?)**

   ...yet doesn't it seem like so many just want to fit in with the crowd?

Questions to Consider:

Have you seen any of these five areas to be true?

Have you ever seen the contrasting complexity that students seem to have with these areas?

If so, what do you think causes this?

Defining Key Terms: **Students**

When referring to adolescents, I prefer to use the term "student" over the term "youth." This is due to a philosophical choice. First, the term "youth" is more of a nebulous term whereas the term "student" refers to _____. The reality is most youth are in school (academic responsibility) and as leaders we must have the goal of each youth becoming a disciple of Jesus Christ (spiritual responsibility). Second, it carries more of a professional approach to the ministry; thus, providing a better chance for _____ with the adult body (who still remember the days of the "youth group" as irresponsible and irreverent).

CHAPTER REVIEW:

o Churched students do not have a strong Christian world view.

o Only 4% of today's students declare a faith based saving relationship with Jesus Christ.

o A large percentage of the churched youth struggle with staying in church through high school.

o There are five social climate areas that are contributing factors in the lives of students (character, components, clusters, chromosomes, and concerns).

What are some areas that you learned, stirred your thinking, or are something that is a "takeaway"?

_____

_____

_____

CHAPTER TWO:

The Past History of Student Culture and Ministry

What is our past and how did we get here?

2

Section Headings:

Learning Outcomes:

In this chapter the student will…

- *Look back over the previous 150 years of Western Culture in order to better understand how the past has affected the present condition of today's student culture.*

- *Look back to see what God was doing during these times in raising up leaders to reach children and youth for Jesus Christ as seen in three distinct time periods.*

The History of Student Culture

Defining Key Terms: Adolescence

Dictionary.com
1. The transitional period between _____ and _____ in human development, extending mainly over the teen years and terminating legally when the age of majority is reached; youth.
2. The process or state of growing to maturity.

Britannica.com
Transitional phase of growth and development between childhood and adulthood. In many societies adolescence is narrowly equated with puberty and the cycle of physical changes culminating in reproductive maturity.

WordNet
1. The time period between the beginning of puberty and adulthood.
2. In the state that someone is in between puberty and adulthood.
3. A period or stage of _____, as of a society, preceding maturity.

The American Heritage Science Dictionary
The period of _____ and _____ development from puberty to the onset of adulthood.

SOME IMPORTANT PRELIMINARIES!

Where and when did this word originate?

"The adolescent grows up to become the adult. The words adolescent and adult ultimately come from forms of the same Latin word, *adolēscere*, meaning "to grow up." The present participle of *adolēscere, adolēscēns*, from which adolescent derives, means "growing up," while the past participle *adultus*, the source of adult, means "grown up." Appropriately enough, adolescent, first recorded in English in a work written perhaps in 1440, seems to have come into the language before adult, first recorded in a work published in 1531."[11]

---

[11] http://dictionary.reference.com/browse/adolescence

Defining Key Terms: Teenager

WHERE AND WHEN DID THE TERM "TEENAGER" FIRST COME INTO CULTURE?

The term "adolescence appeared in English literature around 1440. Adolescence refers to development. However, the term teenager did not appear until the twentieth century. "Teener" showed up in 1894. It first appears "teen" in 1921. "teenager" began in 1941. Teenager refers to the identity a specific group. With the advent of the majority of youth now attending high school, the subsequent baby boom (22 million babies were born between 1946-51), and a nation becoming prosperous, a new culture was born.

(http://dictionary.reference.com/browse/teenage)
Grace Palladino, "Teenagers: An American history" (New York: Basic Books, 1996).

Will this course spend much time on the various aspects of the development of the adolescent?

No. While there will be some aspects dealt with in chapter five this course will focus on ministering to the adolescent instead of defining the adolescent. Other youth ministry courses will provide more detail in regards to development. I would also encourage each student to consider taking an adolescent psychology course.

Why should we study the history of our culture?

Obviously one would recognize that the world an adolescent grows up in will have a tremendous influence on which that person will become. It is imperative to study the history of our western culture so we can better understand where we have been, who we are, why we are this way, where we are going, and what should we do.

> "...men of Issachar, who understood the times and knew what Israel should do."(1 Chronicles 12:32)

STARTING WITH MODERNISM (1890-1945)

While there can be no objective definition to a movement and/or to the movement's timetable, the following is a simplistic description of what is commonly understood as the Modernistic movement. According to www.answers.com many of the given definitions center on the arts. Yet modernism has much more to do with a world view than just a style of architecture, literature, or art. The following definitions are:[12]

Philosophy Dictionary: *"Generally, any movement or climate of ideas, especially in the arts, literature, or architecture, that supports change, the retirement of the old or traditional, and the forward march of the avant-garde. More specifically, adherence to the ideas and ideals of the Enlightenment. This is the sense that gives rise to the contrary movement of postmodernism."*

Britannica Concise Encyclopedia: *"…In an era characterized by industrialization, rapid social change, advances in science and the social sciences (e.g., Darwinism, Freudian theory), Modernists felt a growing alienation incompatible with Victorian morality, optimism, and convention. The Modernist impulse is fueled in various literatures by industrialization and urbanization, by the search for an authentic response to a much-changed world."*

Wikipedia: *"Modernism describes a series of reforming cultural movements in art and architecture, music, literature and the applied arts which emerged in the three decades before 1914. The term covers many political, cultural and artistic movements rooted in the changes in Western society at the end of the nineteenth and beginning of the twentieth century. It is a trend of thought that affirms the power of human beings to create, improve, and reshape their environment, with the aid of scientific knowledge, technology and practical experimentation. Modernism encouraged the re-examination of every aspect of existence, from commerce to philosophy, with the goal of finding that which was 'holding back' progress, and replacing it with new, progressive and therefore better, ways of reaching the same end."*

Columbia Encyclopedia: *"In religion, a general movement in the late 19th and 20th century that tried to reconcile historical Christianity with the findings of modern science and philosophy. Modernism arose mainly from the application of modern critical methods to the study of the Bible and the history of dogma and resulted in less emphasis on historic dogma and creeds and in greater stress on the humanistic aspects of religion. Importance was placed upon the immanent rather than the transcendent nature of God."*

What Were the Contributing Movements During the Beginning of Modernism?

Naturalism _____ (Charles Darwin)

Humanism _____ (Bertrand Russell)

Socialism _____ (Karl Marx)

Rationalism _____ /Empiricism (John Dewey)

psychology _____ (Sigmund Freud)

Philosophy _____ (Fredric Nietzsche)

---

[12] http://www.answers.com/topic/modernism

How Did Modernism Affect?

Science
Government
Religion
Education
Industry
Family

MOVING INTO POSTMODERNISM (1945-???)

According to www.answers.com many of the given definitions center on the reaction of modernism. Using the previous resources quoted, the following definitions are:[13]

Philosophy Dictionary: *"It is usually seen as a reaction against a naïve and earnest confidence in progress, and against confidence in objective or scientific truth. In philosophy, therefore, it implies a mistrust of the grands récits of modernity: the large-scale justifications of western society and confidence in its progress visible in Kant, Hegel, or Marx, or arising from utopian visions of perfection achieved through evolution, social improvement, education, or the deployment of science. In its post-structuralist aspects it includes a denial of any fixed meaning, or any correspondence between language and the world, or any fixed reality or truth or fact to be the object of enquiry."*

Britannica Concise Encyclopedia: *"Any of several artistic movements since about the 1960s that have challenged the philosophy and practices of modern arts or literature…Postmodernism has also led to a proliferation of critical theories, most notably deconstruction and its offshoots, and the breaking down of the distinction between 'high' and 'low' culture."*

Wikipedia: *"Postmodernism is a term applied to a wide-ranging set of developments in critical theory, philosophy, architecture, art, literature, and culture, which are generally characterized as either emerging from, in reaction to, or superseding, modernism. Postmodernism…was originally a reaction to modernism (not necessarily "post" in the purely temporal sense of "after"). Largely influenced by the disillusionment induced by the Second World War, postmodernism tends to refer to a cultural, intellectual, or artistic state lacking a clear central hierarchy or organizing principle and embodying extreme complexity, contradiction, ambiguity, diversity, and interconnectedness or interreferentiality."*

Columbia Encyclopedia: *"…term used to designate a multitude of trends—in the arts, philosophy, religion, technology, and many other areas—that come after and deviate from the many 20th-century movements that constituted modernism. The term has become ubiquitous in contemporary discourse and has been employed as a catchall for various aspects of society, theory, and art. Widely debated with regard to its meaning and implications, postmodernism has also been said to relate to the culture of capitalism as it has developed since the 1960s. …. It tends to concentrate on surfaces rather than depths, to blur the distinctions between high and low culture, and as a whole to challenge a wide variety of traditional cultural values."*

---

[13] http://www.answers.com/topic/postmodernism

I wanted to provide you definitions that are secular in background and nature. The following are definitions of both Modernism and Postmodernism as given from Summit Ministries.[14]

Modernism: *"A broad and somewhat ambiguous term used to embrace a diverse range of arts, attitudes, philosophies, and cultural moods which emerged following the 18th century Enlightenment. Epistemologically it is characterized by a strong belief in rationalism and science as a well as a strong skepticism in both the supernatural and the authority of religion."*

Postmodernism: *"A broad and somewhat ambiguous term used to describe a philosophical and cultural reaction to the convictions of Modernism (which is sometimes equated with Humanism). Postmodernism is the philosophical proposal that reality is ultimately inaccessible by human investigation, that knowledge is a social construction, that truth-claims are political power plays, and that the meaning of words is to be determined by readers not authors. In brief, reality is what individuals or social groups make it to be."*

While the previous definitions provide an "academic" description, they can appear somewhat wordy and potentially confusing to the reader. In his book, *Beyond Belief to Convictions*, Josh McDowell provides some simplistic descriptions of postmodernism:[15]

- *Truth* does not exist in any *objective* sense.
- Instead of "*discovering*" truth in a "metanarrative"—which is a *story* (such as the Bible) or ideology (such as Marxism) that presents a *unified* way of looking at philosophy, religion, art, and science—postmodernism rejects any overarching explanation of what constitutes *truth* and *reality*.
- Truth—whether in science, education, or religion—is created by a specific *culture* or *community* and is "true" *true* in and for that culture.
- Individual persons are the *product* of their cultures. That is, we are not essentially unique individuals created in the image of God; our *identities* are defined by our culture.
- All thinking is a "*social construct*." In other words, what you and I regard as "truths" are simply arbitrary "beliefs we have been conditioned to accept by our society, just as others have been conditioned to accept a completely different set of beliefs."
- Any *system* or *statement* that claims to be *objectively* true or unfavorably judges the values, beliefs, lifestyle, and truth claims of another culture is a *power* play, an effort by one culture to *dominate* other cultures.

---

[14] http://www.summit.org/resources/dictionary
[15] Josh McDowell, *Beyond Belief to Convictions* (Wheaton: Tyndale House Publishers, 2002), 12-13.

To bring these together, previous to Modernism (I will call premodernism) our nation had a _spiritual_ understanding (and respect) for God, a _sense_ of morality, and a _source_ for objective truth (the Bible). Modernism followed with the _removal_ of God yet still having a _source_ of "objective" truth, typically to be found in rational arenas such as _science_. This new period was to bring in an era of utopia. After two world wars and a global economic depression, utopia never came. Postmodernism was birthed in much _disillusionment_ Since God was already _removed_ and modernism did not _work_, what is left? Combine this with new _economic_ prosperity, no source of universal objective truth, a lack of moral _absolutes_, and the importance of the _individual_. This is where our culture is today.

Premodernism	God, family structure, standard of truth being _Judeo_-_Christian_ values.
Modernism	No God, family structure, standard of truth being _rationalism._
Postmodernism	Maybe god (which god?), fractured family (what is a family?), standard of truth is _self_ and _culture_ (what is truth?).

So how does this information relate to the header "The History of Student Culture"? I would argue that the younger generation was mostly affected by the change in world views over the previous 150 years. Some answers are provided in the PowerPoint and some are not. The answers are to get you started and then you can provide your own ideas to the blank spaces.

Topics	Builders (1920's-1945)	Boomers (1946-1964)	Busters (1965-1983)	Bridgers (1984-2002)
God	Revere (Judeo-Christian)	Respect	Reevaluate	Redefine
Church	Denominational loyalty	Nondenom./Organize (church growth)	Experiential relational small groups	Very reactional
Truth (Values)				
Relationships				
Marriage	Lifelong	Divorce	Cohabitate	Why?
Family	Traditional	Trad./Blended	Blended	Definition
Work	Company/loyalty	Transit	Entrepreneur Tech	tech/entry/ what jobs
Finances	Don't trust	trust	Spend/Credit	Debt
Government	Trust	Don't trust	Two worldviews become evident	Answer Don't trust
Authority				

Let's put the history lesson into practical sense, keeping in mind our nation still has a combined attitude of modernism AND postmodernism, especially in education. Enter the fictitious "Lost Larry." Larry is your basic 16 year old sophomore at Central High School. Let's take Larry through … a day in Central High School. (In the blanks, write your own notes, considering the content of the topic, what is the world view being taught, and is the subject more modern or postmodern in content.)

First Period   Literature (_____)

Second Period   Biology (_____)

Third Period   History (_____)

LUNCH!!!   (Then consider the potential social drama of the lunch tables)

Fourth Period   Psychology (_____)

Fifth Period   Algebra (_____)

Sixth Period   Health (_____)

Questions to Consider:

Now that you have briefly walked through almost 150 years of western history, does the past help you see why our culture is where it is at today?

What do you think are the implications and effects of Modernism and Postmodernism upon the youth which have been affected by this world view?

How do you think today's students view:

God _____

Jesus Christ _____

Salvation _____

The Bible _____

Church _____

Christians _____

People _____

Life _____

Property _____

The History of Student Ministry

Much of the material in this section is taken from the book *The Coming Revolution in Youth Ministry* by Dr. Mark Senter III. This is the best work I have read on the history of evangelical youth and children's ministry. Sadly, the book is out of print (or you would be purchasing it for this course!).

WHAT ARE THE THREE CYCLES?

Dr. Senter argues that God many times works in waves, or seasons, of time. This principle is seen in both the Old Testament (i.e. Judges) and the New Testament. As Dr. Senter began doing the research of the history of evangelical youth ministry in the United States, he began to see such a pattern as well. He noticed there were three distinct periods of youth ministry, all around seventy years long. He also recognizes six key ingredients to each of the periods, or cycles. They are:[16]

1. The cycle started amid a period of _rapid_ social change.
2. _Grassroots_ youth ministries started under the hand of the Holy Spirit.
3. An acknowledged _leader_ emerged in the form of a nationally recognized youth _ministry_ _organizations_.
4. Imitators began using the essential strategy _without_ the well-focused purpose.
5. There was a period of _stagnation_.
6. An event _outside_ of youth ministry changed the _environment_ and set the stage for the next cycle.

Questions About Youth Movements

Why Youth Movements Began? *Secularization*
When Youth Movements Began? *Time of Social Unrest*
With Whom Youth Movements Began? *The Middle Class*

(The following material is predominantly from Dr. Senter's book *The Coming Revolution in Youth Ministry*. The italics are my abridged comments. In addition, I have also added some extra material. This is identified with a *.)

---

[16] Mark Senter, *The Coming Revolution in Youth Ministry* (Wheaton: Victor Books, 1992), 70.

THE FIRST CYCLE (1824-1875)

Rapid Social Change

Social <u>dislocation</u> (Westward expansion of the United States.)

Grassroot Movements

- Young Men <u>temperance</u> Societies (1830's and 40's) - *to keep the "good" youth from drinking and negative behavior.*

- <u>Singing</u> Schools - *designed to provide young people a place apart from adults where they could meet together; the beginning of "youth choirs".*

- Young People's <u>missionary</u> Societies - *mostly college students'; raise money, missionary awareness, and prayer.*

- Local Church <u>Youth</u> Societies (1840's and 50's) - *most were coeducational; Baptist, Presbyterian, Lutheran, Brethren in Christ.*

Leader/Ministry Organization

- <u>Sunday School</u> (1780) - *Started in England by Robert Raikes; goal was to teach working children to read and behave properly using the Bible as textbook. By 1785 moved to Virginia and by 1790 was in Boston, New York, Philadelphia. American Sunday School Union started with goal of establishing SS's across the growing western region; more evangelistic and discipleship; thousands established; ticket reward system for Bible memory.*

- Young <u>Men's</u> Christian Association (1851) and Young <u>Women's</u> Christian Association (1858) - *Started in England and moved to Boston; "inner city" ministries designed to help Christian youth who had moved to the cities for jobs; provide place to stay and have Bible studies, prayer meetings, teach character, and be trained as SS teachers; also encouraged young people to bring in lost peers; local churches were involved. William Langdon was the prime leader to bring about a national movement.*

Imitators Without Well-Focused Purpose

None mentioned

Period of Stagnation

- Sunday Schools found it very difficult to provide _leadership_ and _supervision_ of the thousands of schools that were started. Simply became oral _recitations_ and poorly _prepared_ Bible lessons.
- Eventually the YMCA/YWCA lost their initial _purpose_ and _identity_.

Outside Event

The birth of the _public high school_ (1875).

THE SECOND CYCLE (1881-1925)

Rapid Social Change

Social _urbanization_ (Cities rapidly grew; _Industrial_ Revolution; 25 million European immigrants, mostly to cities.)

Grassroot Movements

- _Continuation_ of Sunday Schools and YMCA/YWCA.
- Christian church was _fragmenting_ over fundamental _doctrine_ and traditional Christian _lifestyle_.
- Some _denominational_ Youth Societies.

Leader/Ministry Organization

- _Society for Christian Endeavor_

  - Started in 1881 by Pastor Francis E. Clark.
  - He combined the YMCA concept and the "class meeting" of the Methodists to create his ministry.
  - SCE was based on accountability of weekly attendance and monthly reporting of one's Christian endeavor. Clark began publishing articles on how to get a SCE started. Within 14 years of the birth, there were 56,435 delegates at the annual convention.

- __Denominational__ Youth Societies
  - Many denominations took the SCE program and modified it.
  - Epworth League (Methodists) – 1889; Baptist Young People's Union – 1891; Westminster League (Presbyterian General Assembly) - 1891; Walther League (Missouri Synod Lutheran) - 1891; Young People's Christian Union (United Brethren) – 1894; among others.
  - The Epworth meetings would consist of Sunday night meetings which had a missionary/ministry emphasis and monthly Saturday "sociable."
  - Many of these youth societies developed summer conferences, raised money for missions, developed four year (high school) curriculum, and leadership development.

Imitators Without Well-Focused Purpose

- Birth of __wholesome__ but non-__church__ youth agencies (Boy Scouts, Girl Scouts, Campfire Girls, 4-H Clubs, Boys Clubs).

Period of Stagnation

- Youth Society programs became __generic__.
- Breakdown of connection between denominational __professionals__ and the local church youth society.

Outside Event

The __Scopes__ Monkey Trial (July 1925). (In reality, this event was the culmination of two colliding world views: the Premodernism [Judeo-Christian] and the Modernism [rationalism]. Secular education [John Dewey, Modernism], especially in regards to evolution became the religion of the day.)*

THE THIRD CYCLE (1935-1987)

Rapid Social Change

Social __transition__ (Great Depression and World War II; Secularization of Education; War created a "crusade" feel.)

Grassroot Movements

- First "_Youth_ Pastor" (1932) (Lloyd T. Bryant was first full-time minister to youth at Calvary Baptist Church, Manhattan. His emphasis was "Training through Participation").
- _Youth Centers_ (1930's) (Lloyd Bryant; 40 in NYC area; started Association of Christian Youth Movement of America; emphasized weekly evangelistic rallies.)
- Live _radio_ Broadcasts (1930's-40's) (Percy Crawford; Jack Wyrtzen).
- City-wide _Youth Rallies_ (1930's-50's)
  - Phrase "_Youth for Christ_" was being used.
  - Percy _Crawford_
  - Jack _Wyrtzen_ evangelist crusades called "_Word_ of _Life_" rallies.
  - Jim _Rayburn_ and _Young Life_ Campaign rallies.
  - Torrey _Johnson_
  - Billy _Graham_
- _Campus Clubs_ (1950's - 80's)
  - _Miracle_ Book Club - 1933 (Evelyn McClusky; Bible study)
  - _Young_ Life - 1941 (Jim Rayburn; non-denom., non-church, mostly outreach)
  - _Youth_ for _Christ_ - 1947 (Jack Hamilton; Christian growth to point unsaved students to weekend rallies)
  - _Fellowship_ of _Christian Athletes_ - 1954/66 (Don McClanahan; athletes; mostly outreach)
  - _Student Venture_ – 1966 (Bill Bright; similar to YL and YFC)
- _Local Church Clubs_ (1930's - 80's)
  - Christian _Service_ Brigade/ _Pioneer_ Girls - 1930's
  - _AWANA_ - 1950
  - _Word_ of _Life_ - 1950's
- _Local Church Groups_ (1960's)*
- _Youth_ Ministry Resources and Training (1960's - 70's)
  - Youth _Specialties_ -1967 (Wayne Rice & Mike Yaconelli)

- o _Group_ - 1974 (Thom Schultz)
- o _Sonlife_ - 1979 (Dann Spader)
- o Christian _Colleges_ / _Universities_ *
- Professional _Youth_ _Workers_ (1980's)
  - o _Parachurch_ Ministries
  - o Youth _Pastors_
- _Mega Church Groups_ (1980's)*
  - o Willowcreek Community Church
  - o Saddleback Community Church
- _Miscellaneous_ (1970-80's)* The visible expansion of:
  - o The Christian _music_ industry
  - o Large youth _conferences_ / _conventions_
  - o Christian _camping_

Leader/Ministry Organization (my opinion)

- _Youth for Christ_
  - o Rallies began to stagnate and emphasis went to the Campus Clubs
  - o Campus Life philosophy began in 1962. Emphasized peer evangelism.
  - o Started the "2 plus 2" (Impact/Insight)
- _Young Life_
- Both of these two greatly contributed to the local church. Most "youth groups" became program _imitations_ of the clubs.
- Youth _Specialties_

Imitators Without Well-Focused Purpose

None mentioned

Period of Stagnation

- The rallies came and went.
- The campus clubs stopped growing.

<u>**Outside Event**</u>

The <u>Televangelist</u> Scandals. (This affected [or even affirmed] the culture's perspective on the validity of churches. Christians (and ministries) were no longer to be trusted; instead, were seen with automatic suspicion.)*

Questions to Consider:

Now that you have briefly walked through almost 150 years of church youth ministry history, does the past help you see why our church culture is where it is at today?

Do you see where our "family" history has been a contributing factor into where we are today in the church?

Think about this...

"What About the Last Six Decades of Local Church Student Ministry?"

WHERE ARE WE SINCE "HAMMER TIME" (1990)?

Dr. Senter's book was published in 1992. The following are my thoughts on what took place in the evangelical youth movement during the 1990's and I think Stanley Burrell would most assuredly say you can definitely, well, you know...

1. The rise of _professional_ student ministry (student ministry began to "grow up").
2. The rise of _organized_ student ministry (programs, ministries, events, etc.)
3. The rise of student _participation_ (student missions and ministry emphasis).
4. The rise of student _expression_ (SYATP, True Love Waits, student led campus clubs).
5. The rise of student _evangelism_ (events, personal).

Yet during this time it seemed like the students would come and "watch" the program. The emphasis seemed to be on organization, big & large events and student observation. If you were involve in church ministry during this era, what are your thoughts in this regard?

Please allow me to share some of my own story. The Lord was so gracious in allowing me to be born into a family where both my father and mother had given their lives to Christ in their early teen years and were mature in their faith. They also knew God had called them both into ministry. They both were extremely involved in their local churches and were involved in Christian camping during their teenage years. Both of their mothers taught children and youth in their own churches. While my dad's father was attending church at that point in his life, my mom's father was strongly involved in teaching Sunday School classes as well being involved with Christian Endeavor.

Even before they met both of my parents had approached their senior pastors about starting "youth groups" in their churches where they attended. They both saw the excitement of their local *Youth For Christ* rallies and wanted to have this in their own church. When they did meet and wanted to date, the only place my mom's father would let my dad take his daughter was to the YFC rallies in Binghamton, NY. Ah, let's hear it for the late 1950's.

So when I showed up in 1963, I was born into this ministry minded godly home. My dad was in seminary finishing his graduate program while mom had just finished her undergraduate degree in Christian Education (today's youth ministry degree). They were leading the youth group at their church as they were preparing for the overseas mission work of church planting. I was born into youth ministry. It is out of many conversations with my own parents, personal investigating, as well as active in ministry through three of these stages that I began to see the following stages:

1950's – _Student_ Led
> (Students started their own church groups as they were modeled after parachurch rallies. Many were still participating in the parachurch as their "big picture" place of connection and direction.)

1960's – _Adult_ _Sponsor_ Led
> (Adults began to volunteer to take the leadership of the "Sunday night youth group." Possibly many of these leaders were the actual students a decade prior.)

1970's – Youth _Director_ **Led**

(Things became more organized and began to take on the Youth Specialties feel. Many churches were utilizing young Christian college and seminar students who were preparing for "real pastoral" ministry in this role as leader. Stepping stone mentality.)

1980's – Youth _Pastor_ **Led**

(Churches were now hiring professional staff persons as pastors to students. The ministries were becoming more organized and more separate from the adult body.)

1990's – Youth _Pastor_ **Led/** _Team_ **Oriented**

(As ministries became more organized, the youth pastors added adult volunteers and interns to the team. Students became somewhat involved in the ministry.)

2000's – Youth _Pastor_ **Led/Team Oriented/** _Student_ **Involvement**

(With the continuation of the organization, students became much more involved in the organizing, implementing, and leadership. A greater movement toward relational ministry and emphasis on small groups/home groups.)

Yet I suggest that current student ministry is in a real Identity Crisis!

CHAPTER REVIEW:

- o   The era of premoderism, modernism and postmodernism has had an effect on our culture.
- o   The history of youth work in this nation is extensive and is seen in three eras of ministry.
- o   What took place in the culture will affect the church.
- o   The question is now where do we go from here.

What are some areas that you learned, stirred your thinking, or are something that is a "takeaway"?

_____

_____

_____

CHAPTER THREE:

The Place of Student Culture in the Local Church

What should be the position of student ministry?

3

Section Headings:

Learning Outcomes:

In this chapter the student will...

- *Question if the current model of student ministry is in the Scripture.*

- *Consider if the current model of student ministry is working.*

- *Process through if the principles of student ministry are biblical.*

- *Look at the three needed elements of successful student ministry.*

Is It Acceptable to Have Student Ministry?

The previous chapter concluded with a bombshell thought. Do you have any thoughts or reasons why I would suggest such a statement?

_____

_____

Current student ministry is in a real identity crisis!

Today's Factors Surrounding Student Ministry:

1. _Emergent_ Church Model:
   * it's about the _feelings_
   * it's about being PC (_Politically_ Correct)
   * it's about _experience_ .

2. _Family Integration_ Church Model
   * it's about the _family_
   * it's about being PC (_Parentally_ Connect)
   * it's about _expulsion_ .

Some Legitimate Questions about Local Church Student Ministry:

Is it specifically mentioned in the Bible? No, but this doesn't make it wrong

Are the principles in the Bible?

Should the church even have it?

What is its purpose? (chapter four)

Who should lead it? (chapter six)

Where is it going? (chapter seven)

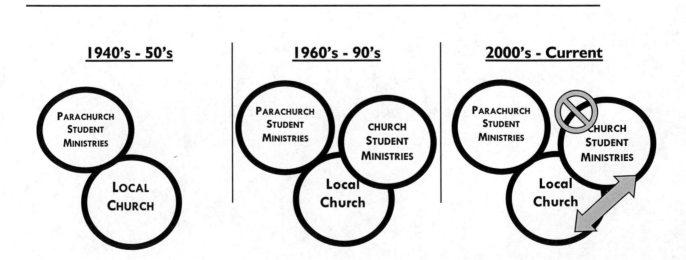

When I started in student ministry in the early 1980's, it seemed like we (youth workers) had a negative to, at best, a neutral view of the local church.

Why do you think we felt this way?

Just wondering if the pendulum has swung from one extreme to another?

Defining Key Terms: Solo Ministry

"Silo" ministry is a term used by some in the church which describes the environment where the children and youth of the church never _integrate_ with the life of the whole body; rather, they always stay within their own _age group_. They simply move from silo to silo. If there is no college age group, statistically they are leaving church altogether upon high school graduation. If there is a college age group, they may attend this group and still may not integrate into the mainstream of the church body. This only seems to delay the inevitable departure from the local assembly. Is this the best way to minister?

Does the scripture speak of **isolation** or **integration** of the various age groups?

Three Legitimate Questions of Local Church Student Ministry

1. Is student ministry specifically mentioned in the Bible?

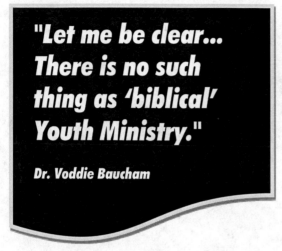

"Let me be clear... There is no such thing as 'biblical' Youth Ministry."

Dr. Voddie Baucham

I am not going to lie; specifically speaking, No . There is no mention of the terms "Youth Pastor," or "Youth Group" in the Scripture. For one reason, there was not the adolescent culture as defined today. For the most part, children went from dependents to independents rather quickly. But what about this quote?[17] Is this a legitimate argument against student ministry? Are youth workers actually counter to Scripture?

In his book, *Family Driven Faith* Pastor Baucham makes the case for the elimination of current student ministry with, as he calls it, three significant problems with today's model of student ministry. The following are his quotes:[18]

1. *My first concern is there is no clear biblical mandate for the current approach.*
2. *My second concern with youth ministry is that the current approach may actually work against the biblical practice of family discipleship.*
3. *My third concern with youth ministry is that the current approach isn't working.*

Pastor Baucham's argument is first based on the notion that because the Bible does not specifically mention "youth group" or a "youth leader," these ministries are unbiblical. It is next based on the presupposition that parents drop their kids off at the church to take care of the spiritual needs of their children. It is also based on the reality that the church is losing most of its evangelical youth. His conclusion is – youth ministry does not work because it is unbiblical.

Response to 1: *I would agree that the Scripture does not call for the church to have youth pastors. Neither does it call for worship pastors, discipleship pastors, or even senior pastors. None*

---

[17] Brian Keith Phillips."One Thing" blog "Biblical Youth Ministry?" http://psalm27four.blogspot.com/2007/11/biblical-youth-ministry.html
[18] Voddie Baucham, *Family Driven Faith* (Wheaton: Crossway Books, 2007), 179-182.

of these titles were in the New Testament. But just because the specific verbiage is not used, are they wrong? (More on this in chapter six.)

Response to 2: *I would agree that the church should support the father being the spiritual leader of the home. The Scripture mandates this! But does this command also eliminate any other adults being in the child's life?*

Response to 3: *I would agree that something is sadly wrong when our churches are losing its youth at such an alarming rated (as covered in chapter one). But is this the sole fault of youth pastors? Could there be other factors as to why students leave the church?*

2. Are the principles of student ministry in the Bible?

I would argue a resounding __yes__! We will take a look at 2 Timothy 3 and other Scriptures later in this chapter and chapter seven.

3. Should the church even have student ministry?

To answer the above question, consider:

- *What is the __role__ of the church to its people? (full __maturity__ - Ephesians 4:11-16)*
- *What is the __mission__ of the church? (__make__ __disciples__ - Matthew 28:19-20)*
- *What about the __spiritual__ need of students (96% are not __saved__)?*
- *What about the __social__ need of students? (children mingled together in Scripture)*
- *Did Jesus __teach__ a Family Integrated Church and/or did he __model__ this in his earthly ministry (Luke 14:26; Mark 3:20-34)?*
- *Why did Jesus invest so much in __John__ and Paul invest so much in __Timothy__ (both teenagers)?*
- *Did __age__ - __specific__ ministry even have a place in Scripture (Luke 2:46-50)?*

Consider:

- *Who will reach the __96__ % of students who are not followers of Jesus Christ?*
- *Currently there are over __85__,000,000 children and youth under the age of 19 in the United States. This means over __82__,000,000 are not reached.*[19]

---

[19] Statistics are based on the current US census reports and the number of claiming evangelical youth.
http://www.census.gov/population/www/projections/ppl47.html#tr-age-youth

- Who will minister to the _32_ % of children who do not live with their mother and father?[20]
- While every Christian father is commanded to teach his children the Bible, what about the kids whose parents are _not_ saved and/or whose dad's _refuse_ ?
- Even for the dads who are obeying the command to teach their children, what about the Body of Christ _benefitting_ from the full array of _spiritual_ _gifts_? (Why would I **not** want the church to minister to my own children?)

What about the Next Generation?

Psalm 22:30 Posterity will serve him; future generations will be told about the Lord.

Psalm 45:17 I will perpetuate your memory through all generations; therefore the nations will praise you forever and ever.

Psalm 71:18 Even when I am old and gray, do not forsake me, O God, till I declare your power to the next generation, your might to all who are to come.

Psalm 78:4 We will not hide them from their children; we will tell the next generation the praiseworthy deeds of the LORD, his power, and the wonders he has done.

Psalm 78:6 so the next generation would know them, even the children yet to be born, and they in turn would tell their children.

Psalm 79:13 Then we your people, the sheep of your pasture, will praise you forever; from generation to generation we will recount your praise.

Psalm 89:1 I will sing of the LORD's great love forever; with my mouth I will make your faithfulness known through all generations.

Psalm 102:18 Let this be written for a future generation, that a people not yet created may praise the LORD

Psalm 145:4 One generation will commend your works to another; they will tell of your mighty acts.

The real question comes down to **who is responsible to teach the next generation**? Is it the home, the church, or the community? Is it a question of _either_ - _or_ or is it a _yes_ - _and_ ??? (By the way, who is the concerned writer of the previous verses? There is a representation of all three in these verses; families, worship leaders (church), politicians and concerned adults (community).

---

[20] http://childstats.gov/americaschildren/famsoc.asp#4

The Balance of Age-Specific, Family-Friendly, and Church-Connected Student Ministries

WHAT ABOUT AGE-SPECIFIC MINISTRY?

Did Jewish Culture Have Age-Specific Ministry?

It is interesting to see the various stages of life that the Jewish make would go through as one transitioned from childhood to manhood. The following points are a review of some of the abovementioned stages:

- *Age 5 – the young child was taught ritual purity as he studied Leviticus and the nature and character of God as he studied the Psalms.*
- *Age 10 – the young boy was taught the oral traditions from the elders and was tested on this material on the Temple steps. (Jesus did this in Luke 2:46-50.)*
- *Age 13 – the boy was now considered morally responsible for his actions.*
- *Age 15 – the young man would study the sages.*
- *Age 18 – the young man was able to marry.*
- *Age 20 – the young man was able to pursue a vocation.*
- *Age 30 – the man was allowed to begin ministry.*
- *Age 40 – the man was considered of the age of understanding.*
- *Age 50 – the older man was old enough to counsel younger men.*

The educator who was involved in the earlier stages of religious instruction was those men of the Jewish tradition. They were priests, scribes, and/or Levites. Within this context, the safe assumption is they worked alongside the Jewish parents as both the religious institution and the home taught their children in the ways of God. However, these men did have a valid spiritual role in the life of the children. (For further reading on this subject, I suggest Dr. Ron Moseley's article "Jewish Education in Ancient Times." One can find this article on http://www.restorationfoundation.org/volume_3/32_6.htm.)

It was in this Jewish background that at age twelve Jesus entered the Temple and dialogued with the teachers. This was preparation for when a boy turned thirteen; he ceremonially became a young man, fully responsible for his own moral actions (keep this in mind for chapter six). It was also at this age that the boy moved to the next level academically within the context of religious instruction. One could say the child went from elementary school to middle school. From the historical background provided, the concept of age-specific education and biblical instruction goes back thousands of years. In addition, Jesus Himself never criticized the system or abolished it. Contrary, one could argue the New Testament continues to use the cultural language of the previous stages. Age-specific education is not a product of a 20th century humanistic philosophy (as many in the FIC movement propose in their writings); it was the model used when the church was born; thus, the Scripture has no negative issue with age-specific education.

WHAT ABOUT FAMILY-FRIENDLY?

The following material is part of what I actually presented at our Adult Leaders Retreat as I unknowingly entered my final year at my church before God brought me to Liberty. This was my commitment to our church and community families.

My Goal for the Coming School Year:

1. This next year my desire is to see us have two _events_ that will help strengthen and encourage our families.

2. I also want to provide a quarterly _Sunday School_ class for parents of youth or pre-youth that bridges me together with parents.

3. I want to have quarterly _open_ _houses_ within zoned areas of our ministries.

4. We will be moving our high school ministry into zoned areas – based on campuses and meeting in home of students whose _parents_ are GODLY examples of Jesus Christ. And within these campus ministries, I want to see _parents_ play a huge role in the success of the mission of IMPACT.

5. I want to see more parents get involved _spiritually_ in the lives of their kids and to see what can we as a student ministry to help parents succeed in developing godly _children_ into godly _adults_ .

How Student Ministries Leaders can be Family Friendly:

- Develop a _relationship_ with the _parents_ .
- _Affirm_ them about their _youth_ !
- _Thank_ them for letting their youth come to the _ministry_ .
- Don't engage in " _parent_ _bashing_ " with their child.
- See our role as _builders_ between child and parent.

How Student Ministries can be Family Friendly:

- Provide __safe__ and __wholesome__ events.
- Not "__overscheduling__" so many events (especially when families want to have family time over holidays) or being out super-late.
- Have lots of __handouts__!
- Return from trips __on time__.
- Provide parent __meetings__, __classes__, family __events__, etc.
- Give __talks__, lessons with the students on how we can have __strong__ families.

WHAT ABOUT CHURCH-CONNECTION?

The church is not an option! Think __marriage__ – Jesus is committed to the church. Think __method__ – the church is Jesus' plan to carry out the Great Commission. Think __motive__ – Jesus loves the church. After the stories of the great builder of the church are told (the gospels) every New Testament book is either written to a local church, about a local church, or to a local church leader. Jesus Christ is serious about building His church; therefore, so should we.

Yet the question arises, should children and youth be involved in the main body of the church? In other words, should our students stay in the silo's or attend the "preaching service"? Consider the following Old and New Testament stories:

1. The Stories of __General__ Assemblies (Deuteronomy 31:12; Joshua 8:35).
2. The Story of __Nehemiah__ and the __Dedication__ Service (Nehemiah 8).
3. The Story of Jesus' __Public__ Teachings (Matthew 14:21; 15:38).
4. The Story of __Paul__ and Timothy's Call to __Ministry__ (Acts 16:1-4).

These examples validate that adolescents were involved in the life of the whole assembly of believers; thus, showing the Bible does speak of pre-adults being in the gathering times of God's people. In each case, children and youth were present during the "teaching time." Therefore, while the principle in Scripture is to have specific ministry times for the older to train the younger (Titus 2:4), the principle is also in Scripture for the *"all who were able to understand"* (Nehemiah 8:2) to be with adults for biblical instruction.

Student Ministries must be about the Local Church:

C = *Communicating* to the students they are part of the local church.

H = *Heartily* supporting their local church.

U = *Uniting* with their local church in mission and ministry.

R = *Recognized* in and by their local church.

C = *Connecting* their students to adults within the local church.

H = *Helping* out in their local church.

THE IMPORTANCE OF THE CHURCH & THE HOME IN THE SPIRITUAL FORMATION OF ADOLESCENTS

At the end of Paul's life, he admonished Timothy *"to fan into flame the gift of God,…"* (2 Timothy 1:6). He next charged him to *"…be strong in the grace that is in Christ Jesus…Endure hardship with us like a good soldier of Christ Jesus"* (2 Timothy 2:1, 3). Apparently Timothy was losing *heart* and wanted to leave his *pastoral* responsibility. Paul invested so much in Timothy and wanted Timothy to know of the *seriousness* of the situation. Paul is soon dying, and Timothy must carry on the work of Jesus Christ (4:9-11).

Over the past few years, 2 Timothy has become my favorite book of Scripture. But this letter, especially 3:10-17, has become extremely valuable. This passage speaks to the need for Timothy to stay on *target* with his ministry. Paul calls him to reflect on his *childhood*, spiritual *heritage*, and youthful *journey*, including both his *home* life and his time with *Paul* in ministry. When one studies this passage, I believe one sees student ministry!

"The Matrix of Student Ministry"

(Paul represents the _church_ .)

10 You, however, know all about my teaching, my way of life, my purpose, faith, patience, love, endurance, 11 persecutions, sufferings—what kinds of things happened to me in Antioch, Iconium and Lystra, the persecutions I endured. Yet the Lord rescued me from all of them.

(The reality that ministry is _tough_ .)

12 In fact, everyone who wants to live a godly life in Christ Jesus will be persecuted, 13 while evil men and impostors will go from bad to worse, deceiving and being deceived.

(Lois and Eunice represent the _home_ .)

14 But as for you, continue in what you have learned and have become convinced of, because you know those from whom you learned it, 15 and how from infancy you have known the holy Scriptures, which are able to make you wise for salvation through faith in Christ Jesus.

(The Scriptures provide the strength to _successful_ ministry.)

16 All Scripture is God-breathed and is useful for teaching, rebuking, correcting and training in righteousness, 17 so that the man of God may be thoroughly equipped for every good work.

The home and the church should be in _partnership_. They should not be in _competition_ but in _cooperation_ . Timothy had a _godly_ upbringing from his mother and grandmother. Paul reminded Timothy what they had taught him. In addition, Paul had a personal _ministry_ relationship with Timothy as a _teenager_ . It was out of this _discipleship_ relationship Paul admonished Timothy to remember the things he had learned from Paul over the years of their doing ministry _together_ .

In conclusion, reflecting on Acts 16:1-3 and Paul's letters to Timothy, one can see the _family_ was present in the nurturing of Timothy. One can also see the _church_ was present in the nurturing of Timothy as he was under the leadership of the church leaders in Lystra and later the Apostle Paul. It was from this background, that Timothy _strengthened_ the churches where he served and brought _unbelievers_ to Jesus Christ.

Defining Key Terms: **Young Disciple**

Acts 16 reveals Timothy would take the place of John Mark. In both circumstances, it would appear that John Mark and Timothy were teenagers. This is noted in the acts 16:3 commentary from the NIV Study Bible, "Since Paul addressed Timothy as a young man some 15 years later (see 1 Timothy 4:12), he must have been in his teens at this time."

While Paul was wise in having a peer relationship with Silas, he was just as wise to have a _____ relationship with Timothy. I find this significant because this is "church approved student ministry." For the next 15 years Paul would invest the good_____into the young disciple named Timothy.

Questions to Consider:

HOME:

What can student ministries do for students with unsaved parents, single parents, etc.?

What about students who don't have parents?

CHURCH:

What about parachurch organizations?

Can they be an advantage to the local church?

Can they be a disadvantage to the local church?

CHAPTER REVIEW:

o The Scriptures are not against age specific ministry; rather Jewish tradition supported it.

o Student ministry but balance with a healthy partnership with the local church and the home.

What are some areas that you learned, stirred your thinking, or are something that is a "takeaway"?

_____

_____

_____

CHAPTER FOUR:

The Philosophy of Student Ministries

What should be the position of student ministry?

4

Section Headings:

Learning Outcomes:

In this chapter the student will…

- *Discover what methods are used in defining success in ministry.*
- *Look into the various motivators which direct student ministries.*
- *Learn a simplistic goal of successful student ministry.*
- *Consider various student ministry philosophy statements (mission, vision, strategy).*

What is a Successful Student Ministry?

OKAY LIBERTY UNIVERSITY! IT IS YOUR TURN TO VOTE!

As An Individual

Think back to your student ministry experience. Overall, choose one number (1-10) which would best represent the success of the ministry. 1= it was just incredibly awful! 10= absolutely amazing! (c'mon, no voting a 5 – be creative!)

"My student ministry was a (fill in the number here) _____."

As A Class

Now as a class, let's crunch the numbers!

1-2 = _____	_____%
3-4 = _____	_____%
5-6 = _____	_____%
7-8 = _____	_____%
9-10 = _____	_____%

Choose the best three descriptive words which would portray your student ministry,

1. _____
2. _____
3. _____

But is success defined subjectively or objectively?

The problem with the above exercise is the basis of success is <u>Subjective</u> – you may be right or wrong. It is typically based on the individual student's experience.

Think about this! You could have three students come out of the same youth ministry with completely three different opinions of the <u>Success</u> of the youth ministry.

> *Social Sarah – she could think the ministry is...*
> *Serious Steve - he could think the ministry is...*
> *Shy Shane - he could think the ministry is...*

So who is right? And is there a more objective, measurable means to identify true success within student ministry? (Hey, and we didn't even mention the opinion of the parents, church leaders, etc…)

Ministry subjectivity can be reduced by defining what it means to have a successful youth ministry and setting the appropriate goals.

What would be your definition of a successful student ministry? _____

_____

Is there a consistent way to measure success in student ministry?

What Guides Many Student Ministries?

WHAT IS ITS IDENTITY?

What Is the Difference Between a…

Youth Group	Student Ministry
■ It's about spiritual a<u>ctivity</u>	■ It's about the spiritual a<u>uthenticity</u>
■ It's about the p<u>rogram</u>	■ It's about p<u>urpose</u>
■ It's about m<u>aintaining</u>	■ It's about m<u>inistry</u>
■ It's about being e<u>asy</u>	■ It's about being e<u>ffective</u>
■ It's about using the students to build the s<u>tructure</u>	■ It's about using the structure to build the s<u>tudents</u>
■ It's about <u>us</u>	■ It's about impacting <u>others</u>
■ _____	■ _____
■ _____	■ _____

WHY EVEN HAVE A STUDENT MINISTRY?

ASK YOUR AVERAGE CHURCH GOER:

- To take care of the _church_ kids.
- To keep our church kids _safe_ .
- To provide _fun_ events.
- To give the _parents_ free child care.
- To give students a _cause_ (social / political concerns).
- To meet _social_ needs.
- Have you ever heard of some of these and/or have experienced them?

Is there a better purpose than some of these listed?

WHAT DRIVES A STUDENT MINISTRY?

SOME REAL DRIVING FACTORS COULD BE:

- What's the _past_ ? (traditions)
- What's currently _popular_ ? (current trends)
- Who are the strong _personalities_ ? (permission givers)
- What about _programs_ ? (denomination, curriculum)
- What about _parents_ ? (vision may be only for their child)
- What about the _pastors_ (s) or church board? (leadership)
- Any others you have experienced or heard of? _____

What should be the best driving factor in what motivates a student ministry?

The following is from my doctoral thesis. There were over 150 respondents, all of whom were involved in some form of student ministry. Below are the results and my comments in the doctoral thesis.

Q.1 Not ideally but in reality, your ministry is honestly determined by (or motivated by):

A)	Tradition (i.e. We've always done it this way...)	13% 19
B)	Personalities (i.e. I need to get permission from...)	18% 27
C)	Programs (i.e. Because my denomination uses this...)	7% 10
D)	Principles (i.e. Everything we do is based on...)	63% 94
	Unanswered	0% 0

"That 63% of the respondents state that their ministries are guided by principles does not surprise the author. As previously mentioned...the author expected this strong of an answer due to the popularity of the books Purpose Driven Church and Purpose Driven Youth Ministry. If anything, the author was surprised the number was not higher. He fully expected more leaders to choose response D). But of the three remaining, it is interesting to note that B) Personalities was the next highest at 18%. This would stand to reason based on the feedback he receives from student ministry workers who struggle with senior leadership and/or church members (including church boards) that determine much of the direction of the student ministry."

Of the four listed what one would you choose which best represented your student ministry back home while you were a student and why? _____

SO WHAT IS SUCCESS IN STUDENT MINISTRY?

Similar to the previous motivators, how do some define success in student ministry:

"GOOD...

- ✓ **A**ttendance   How many _people_ does the ministry have, "decisions" made, etc...?
- ✓ **A**ffirmation   How do the _parents_ and/or church leaders feel?
- ✓ **A**dored   How _popular_ is the leader and/or ministry?
- ✓ **A**ctivity   How busy is the _program_ ?
- ✓ **A**cceptance   How _politically_ correct is the ministry?

...IS BAD WHEN IT KEEPS YOU FROM THE BEST!"

- ✓ **A**pproval   !
  How does the Lead _Pastor_ of the Church (Jesus Christ-1 Peter 2:25, 5:4) rate the ministry?

> **Of the seven churches "reviewed" by Jesus Christ in Revelation, only two did not receive condemnation. Jesus does take notice of His church!**

Defining Key Terms: **Success**

> "My former youth ministry professor, Dr. David Adams would constantly say in class, "Success is 1) discovering your leader's goals; 2) making those goals your goals; 3) then, making those goals work."

If this definition is the template, how does this impact student ministry? In other words, how can one interpret this to student ministry?

1. *Who is our* _leader_ *?* _Jesus Christ_ (Colossians 1:18).

2. *What is His* _goal_ *(purpose)?* To please His Father by _restoring_ God's creations to Himself (Luke 19:10; John 17:4; 2 Corinthians 5:21) and _developing_ maturity within each one (Ephesians 4:11-16).

3. *As His followers, will we* _understand_ *His command to personalize His mission?* The _Great_ _Commission_ (Matthew 28:19-20; Acts 1:8; 2 Corinthians 5:20).

4. *As His followers, will we* _obey_ *His command to personalize His mission?* Our _love_ _response_ to our Lord (John 14:11-12, 15, 21, 23).

Who was the most influential Christian Leader of the 20th Century?

In my opinion, the founder of Campus Crusade for Christ, Dr. Bill Bright (1921-2003).

In 1987 I returned to LU and heard this man of God speak. Afterwards I approached him to sign my Bible. After his name, he wrote three Scripture references. As I looked at the three references, I realized he gave me an outline of not only a potential sermon, but his personal life. Below are the three passages and my added thoughts of what he was communicating .

Matthew 28:19-20	God's _____	(go make disciples...)
Acts 1:8	God's _____	(...through the Holy Spirit...)
1 Corinthians 13	God's _____	(...in love)

1. Purpose
2. Power
3. Passion

What is the Goal and Philosophy of Student Ministry?

This following statement has been in place within Liberty's Center for Youth Ministries for over 30 years. It was initially developed by Drs.' David Adams and Doug Randlett. This goal truly impacted my own ministry and was the catalyst for what I did in student ministry and why I did ministry the way I did. While you may come up with your own mission (purpose) statement I trust the core of this statement remains with you.

THE CYM GOAL OF YOUTH MINISTRY

Based upon Matthew 28:19-20 and Ephesians 4:11-16, the goal of youth ministry is to produce _spiritually_ maturing adolescents, who are _fulfilling_ the Great Commission, by means of a culturally understandable _vehicle_, so that the body of Christ may be _edified_.

LET'S BREAK THIS GOAL DOWN!

1. **To produce spiritually maturing adolescents** – _encouraging_ saved students to be _conformed_ to the image of Jesus Christ (Romans 8:28-29).

2. **who are fulfilling the Great Commission** – _Equipping_ saved students to be _convincing_ their unsaved peers to follow Jesus Christ (2 Corinthians 5:20).

3. **by means of a culturally acceptable vehicle** – _engaging_ students in _creating_ methods which _attract_ students and is _appropriate_ with God's Word just like Jesus Christ (Luke 19:10; 1 Corinthians 9:16-23).

4. **so that the body of Christ may be edified** – _erecting_ bridges by _connecting_ the students to the overall church body; thus, the local church is built up into completeness in Christ (Ephesians 4:11-16).

Defining Key Terms: Philosophy of Ministry

> While others may have various definitions, I would suggest a philosophy of ministry is "built on the foundation of one's doctrine, the combination of purpose, principles, priorities, passion, and the Plan which guide the ministry."

Purpose   – Why we _exist_ (mission)

Principles   – What is our _ethics_ (values)

Priorities   – What we _emphasize_ (focus)

Passion   – What is our _enthusiasm_ (zeal)

Plan   – How we _employ_ (strategy)

IS THERE A DIFFERENCE BETWEEN PHILOSOPHY AND PROGRAMS?

Philosophy	Programs
Who we _are_	What we _do_
Consistent	_Cultural_
Why we _exist_	How we _accomplish_
Mission	_Methods_
Philosophy _drives_ program	Program _reflects_ philosophy
Krispe Kreme Doughnut	Krispe Kreme Doughnut box

Questions to Consider:

Based on what you have seen in your church experience, are ministries program-driven or philosophy driven?

Are programs innately evil?

When can a philosophy-driven ministry become a program-driven ministry?

> ## "Use the structure to build your students and not use the students to build your structure!"
> (Dr. Brown's YOUT 460 work text)

Methods are many,
Principles are few,
Methods may change,
But principles never do.
(Dr. Elmer Towns)

BACK TO A PHILOSOPHY OF STUDENT MINISTRY

To provide an actual example, the following are the ministry statements that I used within my own ministry experience. There will be a basic purpose statement, mission statement, vision statement, and strategy statement. Each of these had core values attached to each statement which will be further explained in the following chapter. Over the years it was tweaked and adjusted but the core of it stayed true throughout the years. As you study this, it sure does sound familiar to what I learned in YOUT 201 "back in the day"! (The name of the student ministry was "Impact Student Ministries." I intentionally removed the specific name of the church and location.)

<u>Purpose Statement</u>

Developing a team of students to IMPACT their world for Christ.

<u>Mission</u> – Individual
(What we are about)

To give every teenager in greater (city), (state) the opportunity to clearly see and hear the gospel of Jesus Christ in a language they will understand so they will become His fully devoted, lifelong disciples.

What is a DISCIPLE of Jesus Christ?
(Individual Core Values)

Out of the words of Jesus, a disciple of His is one who:

Desires Christ above all relationships
who will _deny_ self
who _dwells_ in the Word of God
who is _devoted_ to each other
and who _demonstrates_ the life of Jesus Christ

Vision – Team
(Where we want to go)

To provide a caring community for Middle & High School students which will encourage them to be committed to our impact team:

Together (loving Jesus and each other)
Evangelizing (reaching their culture)
And _ministering_ (serving their church and world)

What do we want our MINISTRY to look like?
(Ministry Core Values)

When people see IMPACT, they see a ministry that is:

openly _welcoming_ as Christ
deeply in the _Word_ of Christ
boldly _witnessing_ of Christ
competently _working_ for Christ
fervently _worshipping_ Christ

Strategy
(How we will get there)

Through the use of a baseball diamond, we **seek to be a ministry driven to draw unsaved students to come and see the people and news of Jesus Christ** (_Entry_ – home plate). Once the **student responds in commitment to Christ** (_evangelize_ – first base), we **seek to develop the student both through godly relationships and Bible-centered teaching** (_Edify_ – second base). Last, we **seek to train the disciple for ministry as we provide practical instruction with ministry opportunities** (_Equip_ – third base). We want each student to see their role as impact players on the team in reaching their generation for Jesus Christ as they go and tell what Christ means to them.

What do we want our TEAM'S CHARACTER to be like?
(Team Core Values)

As we do the work of the ministry, these basic Christ-like characteristics of IMPACT should be in our lives.

People of I<u>ntegrity</u>
People of M<u>ission</u>
People of P<u>assion</u>
People of A<u>cceptance</u>
People of C<u>ommunity</u>
People of T<u>hanks</u>

Even the word IMPACT was chosen for a reason. This word signified the six steps we wanted our students to take in fulfilling the Great Commission.

REACHING THE LOST STUDENT through...

I   developing an <u>Integrity</u> Relationship (lost student sees the <u>love</u> of Jesus Christ).

M   presenting the <u>Message</u> of the Gospel (lost student hears the <u>truth</u> of Jesus Christ).

P   inviting to <u>Personally</u> Respond to Jesus Christ (lost student responds to the <u>person</u> of Jesus Christ).

TEACHING THE SAVED STUDENT through...

A   getting <u>Assimilated</u> into our ministry (saved student develops godly <u>relationships</u> with Jesus and His body).

C   equipping to be <u>Convinced</u> their faith is true (saved student takes <u>ownership</u> of their faith in <u>Knowledge</u> & <u>conviction</u>).

T   encouraging to be <u>Telling</u> others of Jesus Christ (saved student starts <u>sharing</u> their faith with those without Christ).

DO A QUICK REVIEW:

- the PURPOSE is the basic <u>overview</u>.
- the MISSION is <u>what</u> the ministry was about (individual; disciple).
- the VISION is <u>where</u> the ministry should be heading (group; health).
- the STRATEGY is <u>how</u> the ministry will accomplish the task (group, program)
- each statement had a means to <u>measure</u> if the statement was being met.

Thankfully, there are many student ministries that have a similar biblically based philosophy of ministry. Hopefully, this information provides you with an example of what can be developed. I strongly encourage you, no matter what ministry you may oversee to develop a biblically based philosophy of ministry. **Study many examples, develop a team around you, use your creativity, and seek God to see what He has for you!**

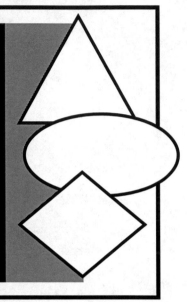

Using a paradigm (visible model) is a positive means to communicate one's philosophy of ministry. For example, in years past CYM used a pyramid. Sonlife used an ascending box. Currently, Saddleback Church uses the baseball diamond. North Point Community Church uses the home. Others use a race track, gears, etc. The point is to develop a simplistic symbol which communicates one's philosophy.

Think about this...

What is the bottom line of Student Ministry?

"Student ministry should be the local church's extension into the discipling process of adolescents."

PUTTING THIS ALL TOGETHER

As a youth pastor, I was committed to the foundation of **correct biblical theology**, which birthed a **correct biblical philosophy** of ministry, which then translated into **purposeful programs** to fulfill this ministry philosophy. My theology dictates my philosophy which guides my programs. Below is an actual case study/example:

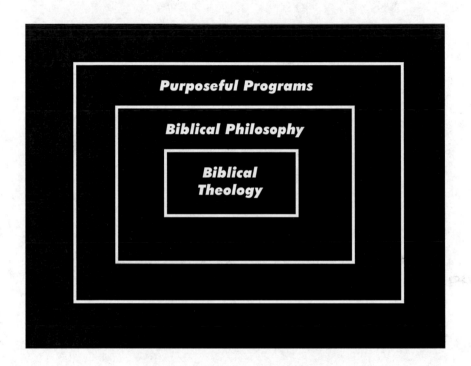

MY THEOLOGY: I believe that Christ's death is efficacious (effective) and available for all. I believe that I am under the commandment of Christ to present the gospel and make disciples. This is my _God_ (biblical) view of beliefs.

MY PHILOSOPHY: This means I need to be serious about reaching lost people and bringing them into a discipleship process. This is my _personal_ view of beliefs.

MY PROGRAMS: Therefore, I will have a Wednesday night student ministry committed to being an open door to unsaved students, a Sunday morning committed to basic growth for believers and a Sunday evening ministry committed to training students to be ministers for Christ. This is my _structure_ to carry out my God beliefs and personal beliefs.

Questions to Consider:

Did your student ministry back home have a written ministry philosophy?

Did the student ministry have some type of paradigms (symbols) to communicate the philosophy?

Was it communicated to you as a student?

Did it truly guide your ministry to or was it just on paper?

CHAPTER REVIEW:

o There are many factors that guide ministries but we should pursue what is best as defined by the Leader of the Church, Jesus Christ.

o There is a difference between a youth group and a student ministry.

o Successful student ministry should have a biblically based philosophy of ministry as its foundation.

o This ministry philosophy should be developed, defined and communicated.

What are some areas that you learned, stirred your thinking, or are something that is a "takeaway"?

_____

_____

_____

CHAPTER FIVE:

The Plan of Student Ministries

How can the student ministry carry out its philosophy?

Section Headings:

Learning Outcomes:

In this chapter the student will…

- *Define a spiritually mature student and discover a means to develop this personal maturity.*
- *Define a spiritually mature student ministry and discover a means to develop this group maturity.*
- *Discover a means to develop this maturity within the individual students and the entire student ministry.*

Developing Spiritually Mature Students (the Mission)

WHAT DOES JESUS SAY ABOUT SPIRITUAL MATURITY? (MATTHEW 28:19-20)

I was brought up with a theology that implied "All Christians are not disciples; you grow into being a disciple. Being a disciple of Jesus is for the 'on fire' Christians." I took it like being a disciple is the "elite club" of Christianity; optional, if you really want to get "serious about the deeper life." As I became a young adult I asked myself, according to Jesus and the Word of God, is this true? In other words, Who is a disciple, When does one become a disciple, and is following Christ optional for Christians? I knew Jesus Christ commanded His followers to go and make disciples of all people groups but what is the definition of a disciple of Jesus Christ?

During my first year in ministry I began preparing for Sunday's lesson. My students all grew up in church and attended private Christian schools. As they told me, they were "bored" with the Bible. In my passion, I wanted to see these students be Christ's disciples. This would be my topic. Yet instead of getting out a reference book or commentary, I simply looked into the gospels and studied every verse where **Jesus** gave the conditions of being His disciple. This study changed my outlook and impacted my life. One of the first youth ministry lessons I ever wrote turned into a series, which in turn became the foundation of my written philosophy of ministry. Out of this lesson came the core of what this youth pastor was all about.

Continuing with this study, I began to realize Jesus Christ did not call people to simply be Converts; he called them to be disciples Being a believer in Christ means being a follower of Christ. This is the terminology Christ used in the gospels and is consistent throughout the book of Acts. Believers were disciples, disciples were believers, period. There was no distinction. Obviously each one must grow in our relationship with Christ; thus, the process of discipleship. With this as the background, I taught these youth what Jesus stated were the necessities of being His true followers.

The Christian life is a process, a journey, into Christlikeness. Obviously one will never see perfection until being united with Christ (1 John 3:2) but each one of us are to pursue holiness (Hebrews 12:1, 14). I believe student ministry leaders must be emphasizing the following five requirements of discipleship and teach students how to apply these into their lives. There is no particular order to these; they are equally important. Here are the five area of discipleship as taught by Jesus Christ. (Of course Jesus didn't use alliteration. I'm a preacher, cut me some slack.)

According to Jesus…a Disciple is One Who Will

D esire_____ **Christ above all others (Luke 14:26)**
A disciple is one who chooses Jesus Christ as the highest relationship_____ *in their life.*

D eny_____**yourself (Luke 14:27, 33)**
A disciple is one who refuses_____ *self in order to totally follow Christ.*

D well_____**in the Word (John 8:31)**
A disciple is one who continues_____ *in the Word of God.*

D evoted_____**to one another (John 13:34)**
A disciple is one who loves_____ *all believers.*

> **We're not going to see perfection but we should seek direction!**

DEMONSTRATE fruit (John 15:8)
A disciple is one who displays_____ *the attitude and action of Jesus.*

Position
(identity in Christ)
vs.
Pursuit
(imitating Christ)

Ephesians 5:8

μαθητής (*mathetes*) means a trained follower. We seek to develop these young followers of Jesus Christ into people that will form lifelong spiritual disciplines_____. We crave for them to "own" their faith in Christ. We desire for them to be true____ and active_____ in their faith for the long haul! We want them to see their responsibility_____ in Christ comes out of their ___ relationship____ with Christ. We long to see them make a _____ difference in their world both today and for years to come.

> Can a student ministry assist a young disciple into deepening these five requirements of Jesus as His follower? _____. But can a student ministry "make" a young disciple grow in these areas? _____.
> Ultimately the individual partnering with the Holy Spirit are the ones to work this out (Philippians 1:6; 2:12-13).

WHAT DOES PAUL SAY ABOUT SPIRITUAL MATURITY? (EPHESIANS 4:11-16)

11 It was he who gave some to be apostles, some to be prophets, some to be evangelists, and some to be pastors and teachers, 12 to prepare God's people for works of service, so that the body of Christ may be built up 13 until we all reach unity in the faith and in the knowledge of the Son of God and become mature, attaining to the whole measure of the fullness of Christ. 14 Then we will no longer be infants, tossed back and forth by the waves, and blown here and there by every wind of teaching and by the cunning and craftiness of men in their deceitful scheming. 15 Instead, speaking the truth in love, we will in all things grow up into him who is the Head, that is, Christ. 16 From him the whole body, joined and held together by every supporting ligament, grows and builds itself up in love, as each part does its work.

Taking a deeper look into this passage, one can identity four areas which are necessary for spiritual maturity. Similar to the "D's of Discipleship," the following are from a teaching series developed entitled "Moving Toward Maturity."

The Head	Be _connecting_	with Jesus Christ in a genuine dynamic relationship.
The Eyes	Be _watching_	and having a vision for service.
The Feet	Be _thinking_	with Biblical wisdom.
The Hands	Be _reaching_	out and helping each other grow in community expression.

The Apostle Paul uses the metaphor of a body to illustrate the need for the body of Christ to be _mature_, _healthy_, and _effective_. The specific context is the _church_ at Ephesus. Also notice the reference for adults to no longer be children but to grow up. This is the process we call _adolescence_! Obviously this text fits: 1) our local churches, 2) student ministries.

Goal	Emphasis
Intimacy (v. 15-16)	Each believer must be attached to Christ both _positionally_ and _practically_
Ministry (v.12)	Each believer must be _equipped_ and _engaged_ in serving.
Consistency (v. 14-15a)	Each believer must be strong in _discernment_ of biblical truth.
Community (v.13, 16)	Each believer must be involved in _positive_ and _building_ relationships within the body.

This and similar series' were taught every few years. Yet the teaching was much more than information, it was designed for application, which leads to transformation! I would share with the group how we as a ministry would provide a structure (program) to help each student develop in these areas.

Three phases of Biblical Discipleship:

INFORMATION → APPLICATION → TRANSFORMATION

Reflecting what has been covered, we desire to see students growing as disciples of Jesus Christ (the "D's" of discipleship) within the context of their local church (head, eyes, feet, hands). But I have a question. **What are some of the developmental needs of today's students?** And does the Bible have answers for these needs?

Have you ever thought of Jesus as a teenager?

"And Jesus grew in wisdom and stature, and in favor with God and men." (Luke 2:52)

The Four Basic Needs of Adolescents:

(One year we sat down as a leadership team to go over how we as a student ministry could assist our students in personal development within these four areas. Write down some ideas how you think a student ministry can provide maturity for students within each of these four areas)

Emotional "wisdom"	Physical "stature"	Spiritual "favor with God"	Social "favor with man"

Defining Key Terms: **Stages of Adolescence**

Early adolescence: age 10-13 / 5th – 7th grades

Middle adolescence: age 14-17 / 8th – 12th grades

Late adolescence: age 18-24 / College age (some are saying it is now even longer)

SIX NEEDS OF ADOLESCENTS

Continuing the theme of the needs of adolescence, for years psychologists have referred to some basic needs that teenagers have. As we process through these, consider how Jesus Christ and His Body can meet these needs.

1. The need of _acceptance_ (do I belong?)
2. The need for _Security_ (do I trust you?)
3. The need for _honesty_ (do you trust me?)
4. The need to be _loved_ (do you care about me?)
5. The need to be _Successful_ (do I excel?)
6. The need to be _Spiritual_ (do I know what is true?)

Questions to Consider:

Consider how a healthy student ministry can help students mature in these areas (student pastor, adult leaders, peers).

Conversely, consider how a "youth group" can actually hurt students within these areas.

THE SIX NEEDS OF ADOLESCENCE AS SEEN IN JOHN 10

1. The need of ACCEPTANCE (v. _3-5_ , _14-16_)
2. The need for SECURITY (v. _14_ , _27-29_)
3. The need for HONESTY (v. _7-10_)
4. The need to be LOVED (v. _11-15_)
5. The need to be SUCCESSFUL (v. _25-26_ , _31-38_)
6. The need to be SPIRITUAL (v. _4_ , _27_)

Developing Spiritually Mature Student Ministries (the Vision)

Ah, the mission (individual disciples), the vision (the group), and the strategy (the process). The pieces are beginning to come together. We want to see students grow in Christ. The Word of God teaches that Christian growth takes place in the _context_ of community. Therefore, to develop healthy students, we must have healthy student ministries.

Whereas the mission focuses on the _individual_ student, the vision focuses on the _total_ ministry. The following description is a picture of a healthy student ministry. The five core values listed are the five purposes of the New Testament church. What one sees in the vision are five areas I believe each student ministry must work toward activating as they grow together as a Body. But there is a warning. While a ministry should provide _opportunities_ for these five areas to come to life, one cannot "program" or manufacture these five areas. They are a direct outgrowth (fruit) of the Holy Spirit's control. In simpler terms, this stuff should just happen! Then consider what would happen when these five core values take place in the life of each disciple as each ones comes together during the weekly meetings!

WHAT ARE FIVE CORE VALUES OF THE STUDENT MINISTRIES?

W_orship_ (John 4:23)

W_elcome_ (Matthew 18:5)

W_itness_ (Acts 1:8)

W_ork_ (Ephesians 4:12)

W_ord_ (Colossians 3:16)

> **When individual students are truly being the disciples that Christ commanded, think what synergy will take place when all of these "on fire" logs come together. You will see a blazing fire!**

These five areas are keys to a healthy and _balanced_ youth ministry when it comes to your various student meetings. (Keep in mind each meeting may only focus on one to two of these at a time.) And yet we must never forget our ultimate goal is for these five areas to become parts of our students' lives as life disciplines. Now let's look at how we can help provide these habits into the life of our ministry through our strategy.

Developing Spiritually Effective Student Ministries (the Strategy)

WHY HAVE PROGRAMS?

At the Center for Youth Ministries, we hold to four basic levels of effective student ministry. This is the "how to's" called programming. But why use programs? Why not just go with the flow? Programs give _life_ to your philosophy. They are your _direction_ based on _rationale_. Programs are important but remember they are only programs. The program is not to legalistically bind us but to free us. If all one is doing in programs is filling a personal "job description" or fulfilling church traditions of days gone by, then one is missing the point of true ministry! The wise student pastor has his programs serve him, not him serve his programs. Programs may come and go. It is the philosophy of ministry that must remain constant. For the church who's famous quote is "we've never done it that way here before", may I lovingly say it was Jesus Christ who brought in a major "program change" (see John 4:23). Jesus Christ bombarded the Pharisees on their commitment to traditions and _programs_ which were more important to them than the value of _people_. And if one is still not convinced programs can and should change, just read the book of Acts! I've been involved in churches with both extremes of either a commitment to "sacred cow" programs or little, if any, organization. Please develop a balanced ministry. Use programs and serve people. Don't serve programs and use people! The **philosophy remains _resilient_ but the programs must be _relevant_.** How we best fulfill our philosophy must always be under the constructive mind of "can we do this more effective?"

WHAT IS THE BENEFIT TO PROGRAMMING?

Programs keep us _focusing_ on our mission.
1. Programs can _clear_ us toward fulfilling our states purposes of youth ministry.
2. Programs will _commit_ us to see these purposes are met.
3. Programs will _contribute_ to us developing a means to accomplish these purposes.
4. Programs will _communicate_ to others the seriousness of our commitment.

Programs keep us _fulfilling_ our mission.
- Programs will help us _consistently_ work toward fulfilling our states purposes.
- Programs will help us _carry out_ these stated purposes.

WHAT ARE THE FOUR LEVELS OF STUDENT MINISTRY?

The following levels are specifically designed for event planning. This can include a weekly program, a monthly large group event, or small group opportunities. Everything done in ministry should fall into one (or more) of these levels for effective ministry.

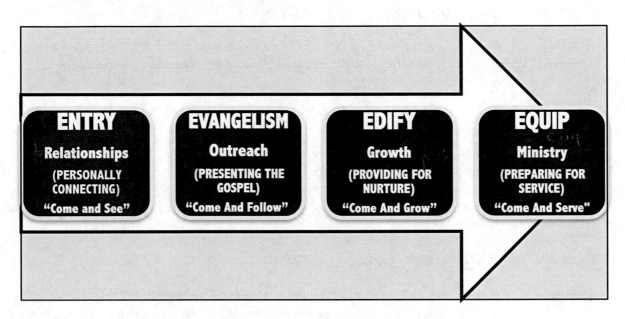

ENTRY	EVANGELISM	EDIFY	EQUIP
Relationships	Outreach	Growth	Ministry
(PERSONALLY CONNECTING)	(PRESENTING THE GOSPEL)	(PROVIDING FOR NURTURE)	(PREPARING FOR SERVICE)
"Come and See"	"Come And Follow"	"Come And Grow"	"Come And Serve"

E*ntry* **level (Matthew 9:9-13)**

Description: A *relational* event - one that *begins* and/or develops relationships with *unsaved* students with the *eventual* goal being evangelism.

Goal: For unsaved students to come and *see* Christianity.

Question: "Can I *trust* in the followers of Christ?"

Examples: Monthly Events (Fifth Quarter, Broom Hockey, Game Nights, Theme Park, etc.), Weekly Meetings (Tradition Youth Meetings, Counseling, Support Groups, etc.), Small Groups and Personal Ministries, Youth Centers

E*vangelism* **level (Matthew 11:20-30)**

Description: An *outreach* event - one that clearly articulates the gospel to *unsaved* students and provides the opportunity to become *followers* of Christ.

Goal: For unsaved students to *commit* to Christ.

Question: "Can I *trust* Jesus Christ?"

Example: Monthly Events (Food Events, Travel Events, Concerts, Rallies, etc.), Weekly Meetings (Midweek, etc.), Small Groups and Personal Ministries, Youth Centers

E<u>dify</u> level (Matthew 9:35-38)

Description: A <u>growth</u> event - one that calls a disciple into a deeper <u>level</u> of Christ likeness.

Goal: For saved students to come and <u>grow</u> in Christ.

Question: "Can I <u>become</u> like Jesus Christ?"

Example: Monthly Events (Food Events, Travel Events, Concerts, Rallies, etc.), Weekly Meetings (Sunday services, Bible Studies, etc.), Small Groups and Personal (Discipleship, Accountability, Mentoring, etc.).

E<u>quip</u> level (Matthew 10)

Description: A <u>ministry</u> event - one that gives growing students an opportunity to <u>Serve</u> and eventually take on <u>leadership</u> responsibility.

Goal: For saved students to be equipped <u>how</u> to serve and given the <u>opportunity</u> to serve Jesus Christ.

Question: "Can I effectively <u>serve</u> Christ?"

Examples: Monthly Events (Seasonal Opportunities, Missions Trips, Ministry Trips, etc.), Weekly Meetings (Leadership/Serving roles in ministry, etc.), Small Groups and Personal (Ministry Teams, Service Projects, Cleaning up around town, Assisting the elderly, etc.)

MOST EVENTS WILL HAVE A PRIMARY PURPOSE WITH A SECONDARY OUTCOME

WHAT GOES INTO SUCCESSFUL PROGRAMMING?

In our senior capstone course (YOUT 460) the student journeys through in great detail what goes into programming. For their senior project, they build an entire year of student ministry, including events, camp, mission, annual budget, calendars, and over 100 topics for their weekly meetings. The following material is an excerpt from the course notes.

PROGRAMMING FOUNDATIONS

1. **Program with the BIG PICTURE**
   - How does this program fit into the layout of the entire ministry?
   - Is this the best day, time and location to use this program in this way?

2. **Program with PURPOSE**
   - What is the specific ministry purpose of the program?
   - Does it fit with the big picture of the ministry?
   - Does it fit with where the group is currently at both spiritually and socially?
   - Do we acknowledge it is expendable and not above being changed or pulled?

3. **Program with a PLAN**
   - Do I have an overall written plan to this ministry?
   - Do I have the basic breakdown for each area to be covered within this ministry?
   - Do I have the specific details written down?
   - Do I have job descriptions written for each participant?

4. **Program with PRAYER**
   - Was this ministry dreamed into existence through prayer?
   - Are we continuing to pray as this ministry is constructed?
   - Are we continuing to pray about this ministry as it has been implemented?
   - Do we have others praying for God to use and bless this ministry?

5. **Program with PARTICIPATION**
   - Am I getting the input of others with this program?
   - Am I surrounding myself with a team of passionate and competent people?
   - Have I empowered and entrusted others in assisting me carry out this ministry?
   - Along with my leadership team, do I have parents and students involved?
   - Have I correctly matched up the right people to the right responsibilities?

6. **Program with PASSION**
   - Do I exemplify enthusiasm for this ministry?
   - Does our leadership team exemplify enthusiasm for this ministry?
   - Do our students exemplify enthusiasm for this ministry?
   - Do we give our students reason(s) to be enthused about this ministry?

7. **Program with PERSISTENCE**
   - Is this ministry being done with excellence?
   - Is this ministry given opportunity to develop?
   - Is this ministry given opportunity to be reviewed and adjusted as needed?

8. **Program with PURITY**
   - Is this ministry being done with all honesty and integrity?
   - Is this ministry being done in a way true to Scripture?
   - Am I and other leadership treating people with dignity and respect?

9. **Program to the needs of PEOPLE**
   - What is the target audience for this ministry?
   - Is the meeting being held at the best time, place and means to reach this target audience?
   - Are people or the structure the essential value of this program?
   - Do the participants in this ministry know that Christ loves them as seen through us?

10. **Program with PROGNOSIS**
   - Are we having an immediate, small scale evaluation
   - Are we having a semi-annual to annual, larger scale evaluation

Now you come up with some of your own ideas

Level 1 – **ENTRY** _____

1) (Middle School) _____

2) (High School) _____

Level 2 – **EVANGELISM** _____

1) (Middle School) _____

2) (High School) _____

Level 3 – **EDIFY** _____

1) (Middle School) _____

2) (High School) _____

Level 4 – **EQUIP** _____

1) (Middle School) _____

2) (High School) _____

CHAPTER REVIEW:

- o The mission focuses on developing a spiritually mature disciple.

- o The vision focuses on developing a spiritually mature ministry.

- o The strategy focuses on developing a spiritually effective ministry.

What are some areas that you learned, stirred your thinking, or are something that is a "takeaway"?

_____

_____

_____

CHAPTER SIX:

The Players Needed for Student Ministries
Who is needed to carry out the student ministry?

Section Headings:

Learning Outcomes:

In this chapter the student will…

- *Identify the value of a student pastor along with his specific responsibilities and needed relationships.*

- *Identify value of an adult leadership team along with their specific requirement and responsibilities.*

- *Identify the value for the students to be engaged in the ministry.*

The Role of the Local Church Student Pastor

THE STUDENT PASTOR'S SPECIFIC RESPONSIBILITIES

WHAT IS HIS POSITON?

Within the first generation of the church, the apostles ordained elders to lead the church. The first mention of this leadership paradigm is when Paul and Barnabas finished their first missionary campaign and "...*appointed elders for them in each church...*" (Acts 14:23). Here are six basic presuppositions of pastoral leadership that I understand from the New Testament which are essential to this section:

1. The elders were the _leaders_ of the local church.
2. Each local church always had a _plurality_ of elders. There is never a mention of "_the_ pastor" (one pastor) of a specific church. Leadership was in community.
3. While there appears to be some elders who held more _authority_ in leadership than others, (i.e., there were leaders of leaders), there was _cooperation_ among the leaders. They seem to have functioned as a team of leaders.
4. There is no mention of the specific pastoral _titles_ in the New Testament that are used in the church today. For example, there was no senior pastor, discipleship pastor, worship pastor, and student pastor. However, simply because these roles are not mentioned does not make them "wrong" or "unbiblical" roles because these roles today are fulfilling biblical _principles_ which were in the New Testament church.
5. It appears there were _teaching_ and _non_-teaching pastors (1 Timothy 5:17).
6. The New Testament eldership (pastors) was _male_ in gender.

One could not think of too many more prominent figures in the establishment of the church than Peter and Paul. Peter was the apostle to the _Jews_ and Paul was the apostle to the _Gentiles_. These men carry tremendous weight as to how one "does" church _organization_ and church _leadership_. From the beginning, Acts 20 and 1 Peter 5 both teach that elders were also called overseers ("bishops" in 1 Timothy 3:1) and shepherds (where we get the word "pastor"). As one studies these pastoral scriptures, one sees these three roles are _interconnecting_ and these terms are _interchangeable_ A pastor cannot pick and choose what role he is to fulfill. This issue of three titles for the same pastoral office can also raise two questions. We will look into both in detail.

Why would there be three titles given for the same pastoral office?

In response to the first question, the reason there are three different titles for the same person is because they all had a specific _rationale_ for the title. By analyzing the Pastoral Epistles, Acts 20, and I Peter 5, one discovers the three pastoral roles are:

M_odeling_ **(elder)**

"Don't let anyone look down on you...but set an example...watch your life and your doctrine closely."

(1 Timothy 4:12, 16)

M_anaging_ **(overseer/bishop)**

"Keep watch over yourselves and all the flock of which the Holy Spirit has made you overseers." (Acts 20:28)

M_inistering_ **(pastor/shepherd)**

"Preach the Word...do the work of an evangelist" (2 Timothy 4:2a, 5d)

Circle the words ***elder, bishop (or overseer),*** and ***shepherd.***

[17]"From Miletus, Paul sent to Ephesus for the elders of the church... [28]Keep watch over yourselves and all the flock of which the Holy Spirit has made you overseers. Be shepherds of the church of God, which he bought with his own blood. " (Acts 20:17, 28).

[1]"To the elders among you, I appeal as a fellow elder, a witness of Christ's sufferings and one who also will share in the glory to be revealed: [2]Be shepherds of God's flock that is under your care, serving as overseers..." (I Peter 5:1-2a).

As you study some other passages you can see these three roles and responsibilities are also integrated into the same leaders. I Thessalonians 5:12-13 speaks of the church's relationship to its leadership as the leadership fulfills their responsibilities to the people.

[12]"Now we ask you, brothers and sisters, to respect those who work hard among you, who are over you in the Lord and who admonish you. [13]Hold them in the highest regard in love because of their work. Live in peace with each other. "

Work hard is one's maturity of the faith (elder), *over you* is one's managing responsibility (overseer/bishop) and *admonish* is one's relational and instructional ministry (pastor/shepherd). Note the people were to respect their leaders and hold them in the highest regard. When leaders do their jobs well, operating as servants and not masters, and the people respond to their leaders in respect and love, living in peace with each other is very possible.

Another Scripture where all three pastoral roles integrate is Hebrews 13:7 and 17. I personally think that verse 7 is to past leaders and verse 17 is to present leaders. As you look at these two verses, the three roles stand out as well.

"Remember your leaders, who spoke the word of God to you. Consider the outcome of their way of life and imitate their faith. "

"Obey your leaders and submit to their authority. They keep watch over you as men who must give an account. Obey them so that their work will be a joy, not a burden, for that would be of no advantage to you. "

While it is apparent that each pastor will have certain giftedness and/or skill set which may lean toward relationships, teaching, or administration, he must fulfill all three roles. He must guard his **godly lifestyle** (_elder_) as he **oversees** the ministry (_bishop_) and clearly **teaches** God's truth (_pastor_).

84

Would the use of three titles become confusing?

Regretfully there does appear to be confusion over the use of the three titles given for pastoral ministry. I would contend that it is directly because of the confusion over these three terms that there is so much gridlock and disharmony within so many churches. Whereas in the New Testament these three titles all referred to the same _person_, in more recent times these three titles became three different _roles_. One now has churches that have elder boards but the elders are not pastors. There are pastors who are not on the elder board. There are bishops who oversee various churches but do not oversee and/or pastor specific flocks. The confusion typically may come down to two questions:

> *"Who is in charge of the ministry of the church?"*
> *"What is the role of those on pastoral staff?"*

I know this confusion exists from firsthand experience in the various church ministries where I served as student pastor. In one of my ministries where I was not on "the board of elders" I respectfully shared the above information and asked my senior pastor about my not being on the board, although I was an ordained pastor on staff. The response was, "Yes, pastors and elders were the same in the Bible but the times have changed." The author would believe this confusion is either due to _ignorance_ and/or an _unwillingness_ to follow the Scriptural model.

With the above as foundation, it is my biblical conviction the student pastor is part of a _team_ of pastors for the local church. The student pastor is to be _called_ of God, to be _ordained_ by godly men, and to meet the specific _qualifications_ given in I Timothy 3 and Titus 1. He is to be a _legitimate_ pastor. While he is not the senior or lead pastor, he is to be the shepherd and overseer to the student ministry of that particular church. With these three biblical pastoral roles defined, the author would argue the student pastor should be that overseeing church leader whom God uses in the lives of today's students. But before moving into what is his role, let's take a look at some wrong perceptions that some (including student pastors) may have.

WHAT ARE HIS PERCEPTIONS?

Some see him as:

- A _Student_ care provider (one who keeps the students in attendance).
- A _Security_ cop (one who keeps the students in attention).
- A _Social_ director (one who keeps the students in activity).

Some think he must be:

- A culturally cool pastor (someone who has it all: sharp looking, played college ball, was in the top five on a reality talent search show, has over one million hits on social media videos, was a drummer in a band and has the best looking spouse known to mankind).
- An internship pastor (someone using student ministry as training ground toward real pastoral ministry).
- A minor league pastor (someone not considered a legitimate pastor).
- A youthful pastor (someone who is close in age to the students so as to "relate").

Think about this...

Does a leader's age in student ministry really matter?

Questions to Consider:

First of all, what is the higher goal of ministering: relating or influencing?

Back in high school, who was your favorite teacher, coach, staff person, etc.???

Did they "effectively relate" to you?

How "old" where they?

Can you think of any drawbacks to youth pastors who don't stay long in youth ministry?

Can you think of any advantages to youth pastors who stay in youth ministry?

WHAT IS HIS PURPOSE?

From Acts 20, Ephesians 4:11-16, the Pastoral Epistles, Hebrews 13:7, 17, and I Peter 5:1-4, one identifies who a pastor is and what is he to do. But to narrow this down to what is his purpose, I go back to the three roles of pastoral leadership. While he must be a man of _character_ (his elder role), the author wants to emphasize the other two areas of his calling: his _ministry_ (the shepherding role) and his _managing_ (the overseeing role).

1. **The Student Pastor's Role as Shepherd**

   - Within his pastoral role of _instructing_ the student pastor is to effectively _teach_ students the Word of God (1 Timothy 4:13-16; 2 Timothy 3:14-4:5; Hebrews 13:7):
     - So they will grasp godly _belief_ (doctrine), which should lead to godly _behavior_ (application).
     - So they will know how to _serve_ the body of Christ (theme of Titus).
   - Within his pastoral role of _relating_, the student pastor is to effectively _build_ healthy relationships with those he serves:
     - He is not to simply be a _buddy_ (just about relationship).
     - He is not to simply be a _boss_ (just about rules).
     - He is to be a _balance_ of both (both leader and friend) as Jesus gave example (John 1:14; John 13:13).
   - Within his pastoral role of _guarding_, the student pastor is to effectively _protect_ the ministry in which he serves (Acts 28:28-31; I Timothy 4:12, 15-16; Hebrews 13:7):
     - This includes _safety_ issues.
     - This includes _doctrinal_ issues.
     - This includes _integrity_ issues (2 Corinthians 8:21).

2. **The Student Pastor's Role as Overseer**

   - Within his overseeing role of _equipping_, the student pastor is to effectively _prepare_ (equip) both students and adults to do the work of God (Ephesians 4:12-16):
     - He is to _mobilize_ the people for ministry.
     - He is to _train_ the people for ministry.
     - He is to _provide_ opportunities for people to minister.
   - Within his overseeing role of _leading_, the student pastor is to effectively provide _leadership_ to the ministry of God (Hebrews 13:17; Romans 12:8):

- He is _responsible_ to God as a steward and will give account.
- He is to _govern_ with diligence. *While this refers to the gift of leadership, the principle is the same for those called leaders.*
- He is _effectively_ to move the ministry forward fulfilling the Great Commission!
- He is to live _worthy_ of being followed (which goes back to being an elder).

Questions to Consider:

Of the three roles, where do you think student pastors are the strongest/weakest?

What type of ministry implications does a glaring weakness have?

WHAT ARE HIS PRIORITIES?

As I entered my second decade in student ministry, I did a personal evaluation of my own calling and the priorities of one being a "full-time" youth pastor! I looked into the Word of God under the different responsibilities of a New Testament elder/pastor and found some great freedom as with God's "job description" of one in pastoral leadership. Notice these priorities are very similar to the previous purposes of elder, shepherd, and overseer. It simply helps organize a student pastor and keeps him focused on what truly matters.

Five Basic Non-Negotiable Priorities of the Student Pastor

1. _Personal_ walk with Jesus Christ (1 Timothy 4:15-16).
2. _Present_ God's truth (2 Timothy 4:2-4).
3. _Pastor_ the flock in gentleness and care (1 Peter 5:2-3).
4. _Prepare_ the volunteer leadership team (staff) and students to be competently involved in ministry (Ephesians 4:11-12).
5. _Provide_ vision and direction for the ministry (2 Timothy 3:10-11; Colossians 1:25, 28-29).

THE STUDENT PASTOR'S SPECIFIC RELATIONSHIPS

TO THE AUTHORITIES (Lead/Senior Pastor, Board, Others)

In Building Healthy Working Relationships, the Student Pastor:

1. Must _recognize_ he is under the leadership of the senior pastor.
2. Must _realize_ this and act accordingly.

3. Must develop a healthy _relationship_ with the senior pastor.

4. Should be _realistic_ about his expectations of the senior pastor.

5. Let the senior pastor know he is _praying_ for him.

6. Should take a genuine, _personal_ interest in the senior pastor.

7. Should be open to being _mentored_ but (with permission) be a shepherd to him as well.

In Building Healthy Working Relationships, they both have needs:

1. The student pastor wants to be _treated_ like a professional and the senior pastor wants to _trust_ the student pastor to act professionally.

2. The student pastor wants _respect_ and the senior pastor wants _reliability_.

3. They both must _understand_ each other's spiritual gifts, strengths, personalities, etc. and must learn to respond accordingly.

4. They both must be _committed_ to communication and feedback.

5. They both should have an open door policy yet both _respect_ the other's schedule.

Some Simple Do's and Don'ts

The Do's	**The Don'ts**
• Publicly support	• Never say anything positive
• Privately encourage	• Ignore
• Invite to events	• Expect him to attend
• Just enough information	• Too little or too much
• Build a defense against attack	• Have an open ear to criticism
• Know when to use him in crisis	• Want him to be your constant hit man.

TO THE CHURCH

1. The student pastor should publicly and positively _affirm_ his church.

2. His philosophy, goals, etc. should be _similar_ to the church and he should _support_ the church.

3. He should be _involved_ in the life of the church.

4. He should be an obedient _giver_ to the church.

5. He should positively _communicate_ with the church.

TO THE LEADERSHIP TEAM

1. The student pastor should publicly and positively __affirm__ his each one.
2. While he may be closer to some, he should treat each one __fairly__ .
3. He should __value__ them as gifts from God and __equals__ in Christ.
4. He should treat them with __respect__ (respect their time, families, etc.).
5. He should place them in the right __positions__ of ministry.
6. He should give them the proper __education__ and equipment to succeed.

TO THE STUDENTS

1. He should __love__ his students
2. He should __affirm__ his students.
3. He should __respect__ his students.
4. He should __protect__ his students.
5. He should be the __adult__ with his students.
6. He should be __consistent__ with his students.
7. He should keep his __word__ .
8. He should keep __confidence__ with his students (when it is appropriate).
9. He should __include__ his students.
10. He should provide an __environment__ that fosters relationships, growth, and ministry.

> **So much of the working environment and relationships will depend on the size of the church, the pastoral staff, personalities, leadership styles, history, and age.**

The Role of the Volunteer Adult Leaders

THE ADULT LEADERS' RESPONSIBILITIES

I realize that many of you taking YOUT 201 will not become ordained as a pastor to students but I ask you to at least consider what role you can play in making a difference in the lives of students.

Questions to Consider:

What if everyone saw themselves as able and responsible for the younger generation?

What if every adult would take the time after a church service to connect with a student?

Who is the most influential youth leader in the church?

A DIFFERENT LOOK AT STUDENT MINISTRY LEADERSHIP

One of the negatives in our age of "professional youth ministry" is the student pastor has allowed the church simply let "us" (the youth professionals) do the work (or visa-versa). I believe **EVERYONE in the church needs to see they are in student ministry.** Students are **NOT** the church of TOMORROW. They are absolutely part of the church of TODAY! While they are not currently in "leadership" roles in the church, they are part of the church. And because they are part of the church, the church needs to see everyone has a part in building into the younger generation. Paul expressed this need to both Timothy and Titus in his pastoral epistles to the churches. With this presupposition in place, what role can each one play? Remember the great dropout rate and our need to connect students to our church??? By using this paradigm we can begin to rebuild the bridge back to the adults in the body.

FIVE LEVELS OF TEAM

SOCIAL TEAM
People willing to <u>open</u> up and talk to students.

SUPPLY TEAM
People willing to <u>share</u> their resources for students.

SUPPLICATION TEAM
People willing to <u>pray</u> for students.

SUPPORT TEAM
People willing and competent to <u>perform</u> tasks in student ministry.

SHEPHERD TEAM
People willing and competent at <u>developing</u> nurturing relationships with students.

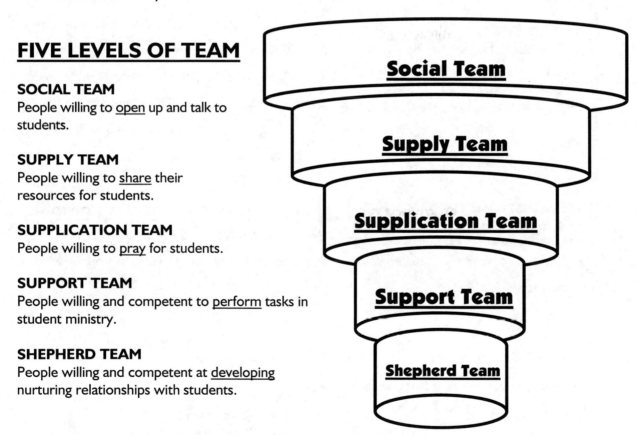

THE SPECIFIC "HANDS ON" TEAM (SUPPORT & SHEPHERD)

As the student pastor establishes the proper philosophy of ministry, he must begin assimilating a team of adults he can dream with, work with, pray with, cry with, and laugh with. If we have a student pastor trying to do all of this alone, or even with a small handful of people, he is not wise and will burn out! God never intended any leader to be a one person show. Take a look at any effective godly leader and you see an effective godly ministry team right alongside. The biblical plan is for the student pastor to _Surround_ himself with godly people committed to the same purpose and goals that he endears. To think he can do the job by himself is foolish, selfish, and unbiblical.

When looking for potential leaders, I sought adults that truly loved God and loved students. While we are all still human, I held high the six Leadership Qualities as described in the text box. Please read and reflect on these. Starting with myself as example (elder), I wanted to see these in each one of our leaders as a lifestyle.

Leadership Qualities

Demonstrate c _onnection_
with Jesus Christ (John 15:4-5)

Demonstrate c _ompassion_
for students (1 Corinthians 13:1-3)

Demonstrate c _alling_
to the ministry (1 Corinthians 12:3-5)

Demonstrate c _onsumption_
for the Great Commission (Matthew 28:19-20)

Demonstrate c _oncern_
for excellence (1 Peter 4:10)

Demonstrate c _ommitment_
to the team (Philippians 1:27)

Upon assimilating the team, the leader must begin meeting with his team on a regular basis for training, planning, prayer, communication, and building camaraderie. Throughout the years of professional youth ministry experience, my greatest legacy and source of human strength were the adult teams God gave me. I will even say my ministry to and with my team was even more a _priority_ than my ministry to the students. It was through these godly leaders so much ministry was accomplished. On a human scale, I was nothing without these leaders!

SOME OF THE SPECIFIC ROLES OF ADULT LEADERSHIP

For the Support Team: (some examples I used)

- Worship
- Drama
- Decoration/Staging
- Transportation
- Events
- Registration (Check-In)
- Hospitality/Guest Services

- Refreshments
- Recreation
- Set Up
- Audio/Visual technicians
- Security
- Data base (office assistance)
- Host homes

Any others? _____

For the Shepherd Team: *(some examples I used)*

- Discussion Groups
- Discipleship Groups
- One-on-One Discipleship
- Teachers
- Campus Group Leaders

Any others? _____

WHAT ARE SOME BENEFITS OF ADULT LEADERS?

For the Students

- It gives the student a variety of adults to _relate_ .
- It gives the student a variety of godly _role_ models.
- It shows the student there are adults who are not "_paid_" to spend time with them.
- It shows the student how the Body of Christ is supposed to be able to _work together_ ("many members-same body" I Cor.12).
- It shows the student there are adults in their church who love _them_ , their _church_, and the _Lord Jesus Christ_ .
- It shows the student it's not only the student pastor who can _serve_ God.
- For every adult the student connects to, each adult gives them one more _reason_ to be connected to their church.

For the Student Pastor

- It provides the youth pastor with the needed workers to carry on _effective_ ministry.
- It creates an environment from which _creative_ ideas, vision, and strategy can be _birthed_ and put into _action_ .
- It provides tremendous ministry benefit as the _gifts_ and _talents_ of many are used for one common purpose.
- It extends the personal _influence_ of the youth pastor much further than can be done by one _individual_ (thus causing the group to "feel small" as it gets larger).
- It provides the student pastor a team to share the _joy_ and burden of ministry.
- It fulfills the biblical command to produce _internal_ leadership (2 Timothy 2:2).
- It provides the student pastor with much needed _relationship_ and guards against ministry _loneliness_ and _isolation_ .
- It generates built-in _accountability_ as he is watched by his leaders.

Questions to Consider:

What do you think are some benefits of a leadership team for the volunteers?

What do you think are some benefits of a multigenerational leadership team?

The Various Professional Roles of Student Ministry Inside and Outside the Local Church

INSIDE THE CHURCH

The following are based on actual paid ministry positions (other than pastoring) that I am aware of. Obviously the financial status and/or size of a church will depend greatly on the availability of these positions. They are in no specific order of importance but are rather listed alphabetically.

- _Administrative_
- _Campus_ and/or _Community_ Outreach
- _Curriculum_ Development
- _Discipleship_ and/or _small groups_
- _Female lead_ to work with _administering_ the mentoring ministry to the female students.
- _Programming_
- _Worship_ and/or _Creative Arts_

Any others? _____

(Please note that some of these positions can also be combined within some contexts.)

OUTSIDE THE CHURCH

Similar to the previous list, the following are based on actual paid ministry positions that I am aware of which are outside of the local church. Many of these may entail the student ministry worker having to raise his/her own support. These also may include Christian ministries or even "secular" positions. Just as the previous list, these positions are in no specific order of importance. Also note that some of these may be done in a volunteer means (for example, coaching in a public school).

- _Parachurch_ ministries
- _Camping_ and Retreat Sites
- _Conference Based Ministries_
- _Mission_ agencies
- _Christian_ social agencies

> "I beg of you! No matter what role you have outside the church, partner with others and partner with the church!"

- _Secular_   social agencies
- _Professional Speakers_   (Evangelists, Motivational, etc.)
- _School_   teachers (private or public)
- _School_   administration and staff
- _Counselors_
- _Athletics_
- _Music_   industry

Any others? _____

> ***Years ago I substitute taught in a Christian school and a Public school. Was one "Christian" ministry and the other not "Christian" ministry?***
>
> Consider Luke 8:38-39. The healed man wanted to go into "full-time ministry" with Jesus. But Jesus told the man his ministry was to return home and "tell how much God has done for you." What is "Christian ministry"? Is "full-time ministry" simply a place one **works** or is it a place of spiritual **impact** with a spiritual **attitude** fulfilling the calling of the **Holy Spirit**?

WE NEED SOME ENTREPRENEURS!!!

Within our first chapter we noted the sad reality of the breakdown of our nation morally and spiritually. As our culture (and families) continues to be "redefined" by a strong secular movement and move away from God's truth, the more the followers of Jesus Christ have the opportunity to "let our light shine" (Matthew 5:16) and be the ambassadors for Christ we are called to be (2 Corinthians 5:20). Here's where I am going with this; for every statistic you read about online or every hurting youth you see in real life, they are a person that Christ died for and God wants to adopt into His family. **I am urging us all to become more** _creative_ **, to become more** _courageous_ **, and to become more** _captured_ **with developing the bridges to minister to these "stats' that are actually real people in need.**

Consider the following:

- For every teen suicide, who will reach out to those left behind?

- For every teen abortion, who will communicate to this young lady that God can heal her grief and pain.

- For every teen that has been sexually abused, who will show this teen that God the Father does care and calls them precious?

- For every young man who is running with a gang, who will be the loyal relationship that they crave?

- For every young girl who just sold herself on the street, who will let her know that God's love is selfless and unconditional? He seeks to free her and not exploit her?

- For every teenager who ran away from home, who will be there to help restore the fathers to their children and the children to the fathers?

- (And speaking of fathers) For every teenager who does not have a father, who will show them that God is the father to the fatherless?

I love the church so I say this with a sad heart. I am afraid the church does not always know how to relate to the needs and even the people I just described. I have been involved in the "behind the scenes" of church life my entire life. I know this from the personal experience of being a pastor's son and being in a pastoral role myself. Churches are typically too tied up with the constraints of the budget and maintaining harmony over non eternal issues rather than tackling what really matters. Please do not take this as one writing with anger toward the church. Again, I love the church! I just would long to see the church move back to the days of the book of Acts where we stepped into the messy lives of messy people and did something about seeing the grace of God changing and healing their lives.

So again I ask; what will we do to be more creative, to become more courageous, and to become more captured with seeking to save the lost? It may be God is calling you to initiate a new ministry, even a whole new method to reach out to those who truly need to "taste and see that the Lord is good" (Psalm 34:8).

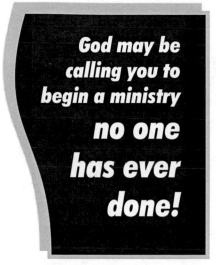

God may be calling you to begin a ministry no one has ever done!

Let us take this moment to stop and pray that God will pound in our hearts His heart for the lost. Let us also pray that God will give us wisdom in how we can better come alongside people and reach them right where they are, just like our Master did as seen in the gospels. I love the story as recorded in Mark 1:

[40] "A man with leprosy came and knelt in front of Jesus, begging to be healed. "If you are willing, you can heal me and make me clean," he said. [41] Moved with compassion, **Jesus reached out and touched him.** "I am willing," he said. "Be healed!" [42] Instantly the leprosy disappeared, and the man was healed. "

How Do I Know I am Called to Student Minitry?

First of all, we all have a general calling to ministry (Ephesians 2:10) and all have spiritual gifts we are responsible to use (1 Peter 4:10). But what about the specific calling, especially as it relates to being a student pastor?

- S tarts in your Heart! (1 Timothy 3:1)
  You S eek it – God's C hoosing

- S kills are placed within you (2 Timothy 1:6; 1 Peter 4:10-11)
  You are S haped to do it - God's C onstructing

- S hown to Others (2 Timothy 1:6)
  Others S ee it - God's C onfirming

- S ituations bring it to pass (Acts 9; 16:1-4)
  God S overeignly designs it - God's C ircumstances

We partner with God! Just like our salvation, our growth, and our calling, we see...

The Human Side:	**The Divine Side:**

Crave_____ nothing but ministry

Gives_____ you opportunity by exposing you to ministry.

Ability_____ to do the specific ministry

Ordains_____ you by examining you for ministry in ministry.

Lifestyle_____ exemplifies a godly ministry

Designates_____ you by equipping you to do ministry.

Leadership_____ verifies your calling to ministry

How Can I Prepare For Ministry Right Now?
(look into the life of Timothy based on Acts 16:1-4)

1. Put yourself in the _position_ of personal _growth_.
2. Be _involved_ where you _are_.
3. Develop _relationships_ with godly _adults_.
4. Take _advantage_ of ministry _opportunities_.

Defining Key Terms: Student Involvement

How important are the students in student ministry?
The students are your players. Without them you have no ministry!!!

Consider a healthy student ministry is like an athletic team:
Head coach – student pastor
(Provides _overall_ leadership, direction, and stability)
Assistant coaches – adult leadership
(Provides _specific_ instruction and relationship)
Players – students
(Provide the _means_ to make it happen! A team cannot win without players!)

Questions to Consider:

Am I willing to seek God for my place in student ministry?

Do I sense a calling to student ministry?

Do I understand it is not based on emotions, feelings, guilt, or even need but on God's calling?

CHAPTER REVIEW:

o God has a specific order for church leadership and a pastoral calling and responsibility is to be taken seriously.

o A student pastor should be mindful of the seriousness of his maturity, ministry and managing.

o Students Pastors must be wise in building effective leadership teams.

o There are a significant number of opportunities within student ministry.

o All believers are called to ministry but there are those who have a specific calling into vocational ministry.

What are some areas that you learned, stirred your thinking, or are something that is a "takeaway"?

_____

_____

_____

CHAPTER SEVEN:

The Priorities of Student Ministry

What is the big picture of student ministry?

7

Section Headings:

Learning Outcomes:

In this chapter the student will...

- *Learn the three categories of priorities within student ministries.*
- *Look into 2 Timothy 3:14-17 to see what is needed to help keep students strong in their faith.*
- *Review what has been learned in the course and see what CYM seeks to accomplish in the lives of its students.*

Basic Priorities for a Healthy Student Ministry

I trust you have understood by now that God is concerned for a healthy church; thus, a healthy student ministry. The following material is necessary components which can assist a student ministry in guarding its priorities, direction and evaluation.

The Ten Ministry Priorities of Student Ministry
What Should A Student Ministry Should Be About

- _Spiritual_ ministry (stemming from a genuine need for God)
- _Biblical_ ministry (based on the teaching and obeying of God's Word)
- _Familial_ ministry (valuing and building of the family)
- _Relational_ ministry (people connecting with people, including the church)
- _Pastoral_ ministry (led by leadership that is called, passionate, and trained)
- _Intentional_ ministry (everything is done with purpose)
- _Professional_ ministry (providing an organized and mature ministry)
- _Cultural_ ministry (understanding of the culture to reach the culture)
- _Developmental_ ministry (moving people along in spiritual growth)
- _Foundational_ ministry (the big picture of a lifetime of godliness)

Defining the Ten Priorities

Spiritual ministry
- _Worships_ and _respects_ God in spirit and truth
- _Seeks_ God through _prayer_ and is led by God

Biblical ministry
- Bases all _beliefs_ and _values_ on Scripture
- Teaches the Word of God _accurately_, completely, _understandably_, and practically

Familial ministry
- Values the _position_ and the _authority_ of the home
- Encourages and _builds_ the family

Relational ministry

- Values ___people___ as God's highest creation
- Connects students to ___peers___, adult leaders, and the overall ___church___ body

Pastoral ministry

- Led by a professional leader that ___called___, godly, ___passionate___, and trained
- Understands and values the importance of building a ___team___

Intentional ministry

- Plans and ___provides___ everything according to the stated purpose
- Evaluates the ministry to further greater ___effectiveness___

Professional ministry

- Provides a ___mature___ and ___stable___ ministry
- Provides an effective ___organization___ to fulfill its purpose

Cultural ministry

- Understands the current culture in order to best ___articulate___ to and ___reach___ the culture
- Works within the current culture of the ___local___ church in order to build the church

Developmental ministry

- Moves people along through the various ___stages___ of spiritual maturity
- Uses ___group___ teaching, ___small___ groups, and ___personal___ discipleship

Foundational ministry

- Prepares the student to have a ___lifelong___ personal, authentic life in Christ
- Transitions the student into healthy adult relationships in the ___church___ and the ___community___

The Five Relational Priorities of Student Ministry

A student ministry should be connecting students with ___Jesus Christ___, their ___families___, their ___ministry___, their ___church___, and their ___generation___.

The Five Principled Priorities of Student Ministry

Christ-centered, purpose-driven, family-friendly, team-oriented, church-connected

Keeping Our Students Engaged for the Long Haul

As stated in Chapter One, there is a real tragedy of student leaving the church. This is unacceptable. The church must begin to stop the bleeding or the body will eventually die. Will you join me in helping us keep our students connected to the Vine?

- While I am obviously concerned about the _lost_ 96%...
- We must stop _losing_ our own.
- I think the real _tragedy_ is the departure of the churched youth. If we cannot keep them, what good is it to keep _reaching_ more?
- I believe they are the _players_ to reach their generation! If the players are not _healthy_, on the _inactive_ roster, or just stopped _being_ on the team, how will we win?

As pointed out in chapter three, I believe 2 Timothy 3:10-17 has the solution. We took a look at this passage in relation to the church and the home being positive partners in ministering to the students. Looking back at this passage, one can also see the solution to keep students who are tempted to drift away. After all, this is why Paul wrote this passage. Timothy wanted to quit "church" and the ministry. After all, Demas just did (2 Timothy 4:10). The following material is from an outline I put together for various church speaking opportunities on this subject. It is so exciting for me to see that God's Word absolutely contains the answers. Below is 2 Timothy 3:10-17

10 "You, however, know all about my teaching, my way of life, my purpose, faith, patience, love, endurance, 11 persecutions, sufferings—what kinds of things happened to me in Antioch, Iconium and Lystra, the persecutions I endured. Yet the Lord rescued me from all of them. 12 In fact, everyone who wants to live a godly life in Christ Jesus will be persecuted, 13 while evil men and impostors will go from bad to worse, deceiving and being deceived. 14 But as for you, continue in what you have learned and have become convinced of, because you know those from whom you learned it, 15 and how from infancy you have known the holy Scriptures, which are able to make you wise for salvation through faith in Christ Jesus. 16 All Scripture is God-breathed and is useful for teaching, rebuking, correcting and training in righteousness, 17 so that the man of God may be thoroughly equipped for every good work."

"What's Up With Our Churched Students?"

Why are we losing them?

Give some of your reasons why you think?

Are they saved, scriptural, : serving?

_____

How can we keep them?

Give some of your suggestions how we can keep them

_____

_____

"Why Are We Losing Them?"

- ✓ Are they _Saved_ ?
- ✓ Are they _Scriptural_ ?
- ✓ Are they _Serving_ ?

2 Timothy 3:10-17

Verse 14 IS Student Ministry!!!

"But as for you, _continue_ in what you have _learned_ (what-doctrine) and have become _convinced_ of (why-apologetics), because you _know those_ (how-intentional godly relationships) from whom you learned it."

"How Can We Keep Them?" We need to make sure…

- ✓ **Our students are g_enuinely_ S_aved_ ! (v.15)**
  "and how from infancy you have known the holy Scriptures, which are able to make you wise for salvation through faith in Christ Jesus."

- ✓ **Our students are g_rounded_ in S_cripture_ ! (v.16)**
  "All Scripture is God-breathed and is useful for teaching, rebuking, correcting and training in righteousness,"

- ✓ **Our students are g_iving_ through S_erving_ ? (v.17)**
  "so that the man of God may be thoroughly equipped for every good work."

1. **Sources:**

- Students need both _church_ & _home_ .
- Both the home and church must build _godly_ , _intentional_ relationships.

2. **Scriptures:**

- Teach students to _know_ God's Word (_doctrine_).
- Teach students to _trust_ God's Word (_apologetics_).
- Teach students to _apply_ God's Word (_application_).

3. **Salvation:**

- Make sure the students are genuinely _saved_ .
- Salvation must lead to godly living and _ministry_ .

4. **Service:**

- With these foundations in place our students can become effective _servants_ of King Jesus!

In conclusion, there is no "guaranteed" means of student ministry workers making sure each student is a lifelong follower of Jesus Christ (after all, Demas left Paul). As stated in chapter five, "ultimately the individual partnering with the Holy Spirit are the ones to work this out (Philippians 1:6; 2:12-13)." Yet if we provide a ministry that obeys these principles as given by the Apostle Paul, I believe our chances are extremely strong.

In case you are wondering, Timothy finished with Christ and finished strong.

Reviewing the Course and Closing Thoughts

Chapter 1   The Present Condition of Student Culture

This chapter introduced us to the reality of the spiritual and social climate of today's students. Well over 90% of the generation is not saved and the church loses the majority of it own youth. We looked into the character, components, clusters, and conduct, and concerns.

Chapter 2   The Past History of Student Culture and Ministry

We examined the history of western culture, especially its relation to modernism and postmodernism, and how this affected the student culture. We took an extensive look into the history of student ministry by looking into the three cycles of the student ministry movement.

Chapter 3   The Place of Student Ministry in the Local Church

This chapter focused on the current identity crisis of student ministry, especially as it related to the biblical credibility of age-specific ministries.

Chapter 4   The Philosophy of Student Ministry

Within this chapter we examined what criteria are used to define success in ministry. In relation to philosophy, we examined the stated goal of student ministry and the ensuing mission, vision, and strategy statements.

Chapter 5   The Plan of Student Ministry

The emphasis within this chapter was on the actual approach of fulfilling the philosophy. Attention was given to the six "D's of Discipleship" (the mission), the five "W's of the Church" (the vision), and the four levels of ministry (the strategy).

Chapter 6   The Players Needed in Student Ministries

This chapter provided a biblical definition of the role of a pastor, especially as it relates to a student pastor in his responsibilities and relationships. We also learned about the need for a competent leadership team to assist in carrying out the ministry.

Chapter 7   The Priorities of Student Ministries

In this chapter we saw a closing overview of the course by seeing three listings of needed priorities. The chapter took note of 2 Timothy 3:14-17 as an outline to assist student in staying strong in their lives. We also reviewed what has been learned in the course and see what CYM seeks to accomplish in the lives of its students.

And in conclusion...

The benefit of a ministry based on a biblical direction for its mission, vision, and strategy is we are doing the work of our Lord with the clear conscience of a wise steward (Acts 20:26-27). The rewards are the lives that are impacted for Jesus Christ (Philippians 4:1). And the joy will come when we stand together; side by side with those we gave our lives to in ministry, as we experience the Lamb of God together *"in the presence of our Lord Jesus when He comes...you are our glory and joy."* (1 Thess.2:19-20).

In conclusion, please do not think I have all of the answers on ministering to teenagers. Hardly!!! The longer I have ministered to them, the less I feel I know. Please understand I simply want you to see the desire of my life as given in my favorite Scripture, Colossians 1:28-29, *"We proclaim him, admonishing and teaching everyone with all wisdom, so that we may present everyone perfect in Christ. To this end I labor, struggling with all his energy, which so powerfully works in me."*

People of Character:
- goal - each student demonstrates godly living (1 Timothy 3 : Titus1)
- measured - spiritual accountability : peers : elders

People of Calling
- goal - each student demonstrates a calling
- measured - actively involved in a supervisory fashion w/ local student ministries

People of Competence
- goal - demonstrating a goal to excellence.
- measured - sets : maintains tangible evidence of goals : efforts (i.e. GPA)

201: have a biblical philosophy
301: develop a foundation
350: reaching students in their culture
447: discipling students
448: communicating God's truth
450: preparing the leader to be a professional
460: Equipping leaders to be structured.